Mystic Seafarer's Trail

A humorous and historical look at the haunts and homes of Mystic's famous sea voyagers—living and dead—and includes little-known details about Amelia Earhart's secret wedding in Noank.

REVIEWS

"You will laugh out loud at Lisa's adventures in this part travel guide, part historical reference and completely hilarious tale."
Bree Shirvell, Editor, Stonington-Mystic Patch

"With a keen, self-deprecating wit, Saunders tells the tale of each of the 7 Wonders [of Mystic], beginning with Wonder #1, the whaleship *Charles W. Morgan*." *Windcheck* magazine

"Lisa Saunders has written an engaging and solidly researched narrative which should capture the attention of all who are interested in early New England history and the traditions of the sea that were one of its foundations."
David S. Martin, Ph.D., Professor/Dean Emeritus, Gallaudet University, Washington, DC

"Author Lisa Saunders has mastered the art/science/gift of writer-reader communication. She's not writing at you; she's talking to you...no holds barred. Her frequently disarming candor evokes reader reactions ranging from chuckle to head-shaking laughter. " George Nammack, *Long Island Boating World*

"I laughed out loud on a number of occasions. It's interesting, humorous and touching."
Glenn Gordinier, author of *Surfing Cold Water: A New Englander's Off-Season Obsession*

"This book is a splendid way to tie Mystic's history to life today—a bridge from the past to the present—for any age." Lou Allyn, Masons Island[i]

"An historical—and sometimes hysterical—look at Mystic. I can't wait to visit!"
Marianne Greiner, Illustrator, New York

"I found Lisa's anticipation of her sailing adventure just plain entertaining and could relate to her internal dialogue, misgivings, and somewhat grandiose fantasies. She is a person worth spending time with." Ann Kuehner, LCSW

"Entertaining, witty, informative—and cute! It covers a range of topics from personal loss to finding life, history and new friends."
Kristin Hartnett, Executive Director, Laughworks, Mystic, Connecticut

"What a read—fascinating!" Kathleen Poole, former Chesapeake Bay waterwoman

Mystic Seafarer's Trail

Secrets behind the 7 Wonders, Titanic's Shoes, Captain Sisson's Gold, and Amelia Earhart's Wedding

While searching for the Seven Wonders of Mystic, Connecticut, with her beagle/basset hound, author Lisa Saunders uncovers the secrets behind the *Titanic's* shoes, Amelia Earhart's Noank wedding and Captain Sisson's hunt for gold. But will she ever find an adventure of her own—one that will make her thin and famous? Then it happens: when walking the Mystic Seafarer's Trail (which she designed for those who don't like to go uphill), she meets a blind sailor who invites her on a long winter voyage. Can this landlubber defy squalls, scurvy, and her fear of scraping barnacles to survive this epic journey?

Lisa Saunders with her beagle/basset hound, Bailey, on Misquamicut Beach, RI.

Mystic Seafarer's Trail

Secrets behind the 7 Wonders, *Titanic's* Shoes, Captain
Sisson's Gold, and Amelia Earhart's Wedding

Lisa M. Saunders

Image credits:
Cover photo taken by Lisa Saunders while sailing from Stonington to Mystic.
Headshot of Lisa Saunders by Cindy Barry.
Photo of Lisa with hound Bailey on beach by James P. Saunders.
Photo of Cindy Modzelewski and Elizabeth Saede by Becky Modzelewski
Photo of Lisa and Jules by Enrique C. Jograj, Jr.
Pirate sketch by Suzanne Doukas Niermeyer.
Photographs of featured points of interest, including Gloria the cranky goose, by Lisa Saunders
Mystic Seafarer's Trail Map adapted from *Landmarks You Must Visit in Southeast Connecticut* by Constant Waterman.
Illustration from *Ride a Horse, Not an Elevator* by Marianne Greiner

DEDICATION

To all who have been lost at sea.

"7 Wonders of Mystic" * & other wonders

1. ***Mystic Aquarium's "Crowns"**
2. Olde Mistick Village duck pond (where Gloria the cranky goose reigned)
3. Mystic & Shoreline Visitor Information Center
4. ***Elm Grove Cemetery Arch**
5. ***Mystic Seaport's Whaleship, *Charles W. Morgan***
6. ***Mystic River Drawbridge** (seen in film, *Mystic Pizza*)
7. Captain's Row (Gravel St.) & River Rd—views of captain homes, ships & nature
8. ***Mystic Pizza Restaurant** (inspired *Mystic Pizza* movie)
9. Captain Daniel Packer Inne (feel like a character in *Moby Dick*)
10. Mystic Railroad Swing Bridge (will it close in time for next train?)
11. Portersville Academy, 1839 schoolhouse (C)
12. Record-breaking Cape Horn rounder, Captain Joseph Holmes (#77 private home)
13. Union Baptist Church (chime songs at 12 & 6 p.m.)
14. Mystic & Noank Library -Voted 8th Wonder (Emily the Library Cat buried there)
15. Octagon house (#8 private home)
16. Captain Peter E. Rowland, maker of record-breaking run on famous clipper, *David Crockett* (#10 private home)
17. Gold Rush Captain Sisson (#12 private home)
18. ***Mystic Depot** Welcome Center & Greater Mystic Chamber of Commerce
19. ***Hanging Gardens of Enders Island** (St. Edmund's Retreat & home of St. Edmund's withered arm)
20. Denison Pequotsepos Nature Center
21. Denison Homestead Museum (built 1717)
22. Captain Palmer House (discovered Antarctica on Mystic-built sloop, *Hero*)
23. Stonington Lighthouse Museum (Stonington Historical Society)
24. Amelia Earhart's Wedding site (private home on Church St.)
25. Latham/Chester Store (Earhart wedding plaque)
26. Sylvan Street Museum (Noank Historical Society)
38. Carson's Variety Store (locals have eaten there for over a century)
55. Cannon Square (War of 1812). Seen in movie *Hope Springs* with Meryl Streep
B. Mystic Community Bikes (free bike use)
C. Mystic River Historical Society
M. Sunken *Marmion*, mast still seen
F. Stonington Fishermen's Memorial & CT's last remaining commercial fishing fleet

(The maps are not to scale and were adapted from *Landmarks You Must Visit in Southeast Connecticut* by Constant Waterman.) More info: mysticseafarerstrail.com

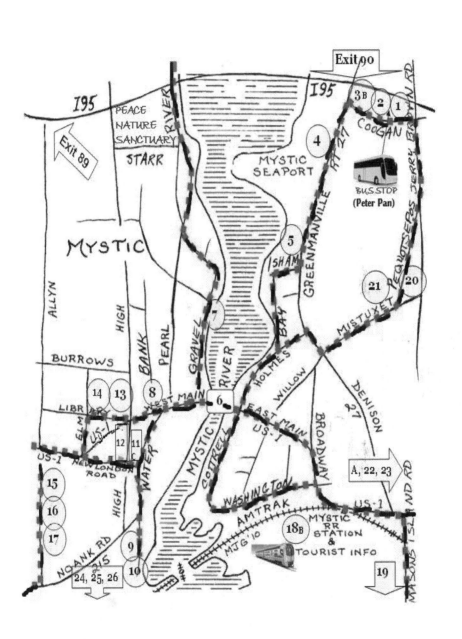

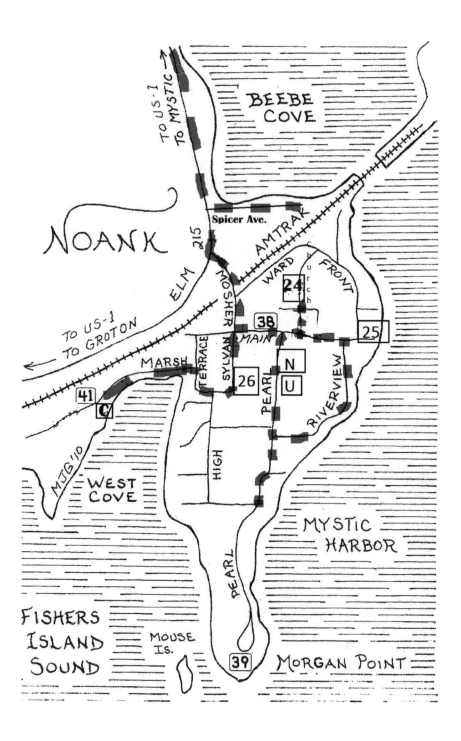

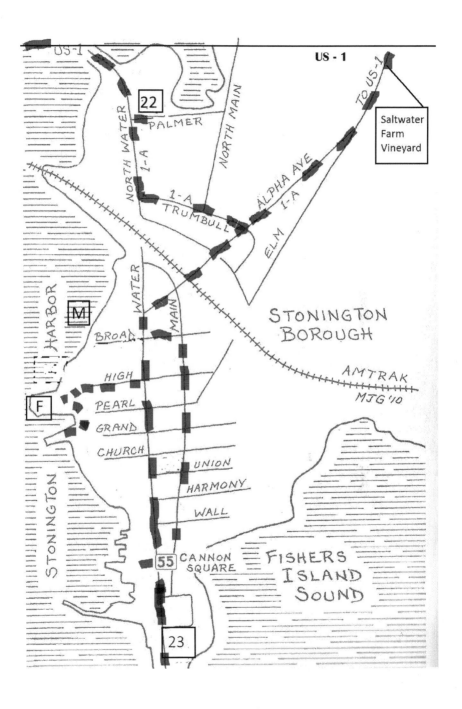

CONTENTS

ACKNOWLEDGMENTS

Thank you to all the living who advised me and the dead who inspired me. (I'm too scared to type my long list of helpers and accidentally leave someone out!)

There were countless Mystic residents who told me where to find fun facts, and many who helped with the editing. I must, however, specifically thank my kayaking friend Cindy Modzelewski. She read and reread this book to proofread my endless changes and encouraged me to press on until its completion. In addition, Mary Moriarty gave valuable editing suggestions for formatting the content and said nice things to soften me before slashing out parts dear to my heart (I managed to sneak those parts back in by including them in Endnotes). Others who gave of their time and information are mentioned within the story or their work is included in my bibliography. My husband, Jim Saunders, should also be thanked for his 30 years of supporting my crazy schemes to find a good story. And, I want to thank you, Dear Reader, for coming along with me in my fact-finding mission and adventure that follows.

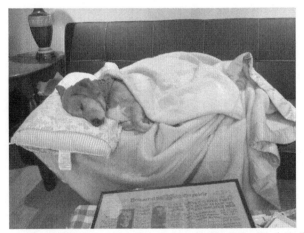

Lisa's hound Bailey rests after a long trek on the Mystic Seafarer's Trail

Since writing can often be a lonely business, I'm also thankful that I had my beagle/basset hound to keep me company in my home office. On the coffee table in front of him is my framed 1930 newspaper article reporting the plight of famous explorer and pilot Admiral Richard E. Byrd when trapped in the Antarctic after his history-making flight over the South Pole. Byrd had come to Stonington, Connecticut (near Mystic), to visit the home of Antarctica discoverer Captain Nathaniel B. Palmer to study his papers before making his historic flight.

1 WANTED: EPIC ADVENTURE

Shortly after stepping out of my new home with my hound for our first stroll through the historic seacoast village of Mystic, Connecticut, a woman pulled over in her van and yelled, "Excuse me."

Assuming she was a tourist wanting directions to Mystic Pizza or some other attraction, I wasn't prepared for what she really wanted to know.

"Do you realize the back of your skirt is tucked into your underwear?"

What a debut in my new hometown—I don't think this is what *National Geographic* meant when they named Mystic one of the top 100 adventure towns in the United States.

Once recovered from my wardrobe "malfunction," I continued toward downtown Mystic with Bailey, a beagle/basset hound mix, to embark on a new life and shake off my old, sedentary landlubbing ways.

No longer did I want to be known as the lady who always talks about losing weight but never does it. No longer would I sit around daydreaming about becoming thin and famous so I could hire someone else to clean my house. I had a real shot at it now that I lived in a place where I couldn't help but fall into a swash-buckling adventure—the kind that might inspire me to write a bestseller.

Straddling both sides of the Mystic River in the towns of Groton and Stonington, the village of Mystic takes its name from an Indian word, "river running to the sea." With its scenic views of tall ships, islands, lighthouses, and secluded coves, it has attracted such legendary honeymooners as Humphrey Bogart and Lauren Bacall. It is a place where those who cross the oceans gather to swap stories and repair their boats. It is where famous explorers are born, visit, get married, or come to live.

To launch my career as an adventuress, I decided to walk Bailey to the haunts and homes of such celebrated adventurers as Amelia Earhart, the first woman to fly solo across the Atlantic; Dr. Robert Ballard, the discoverer of *Titanic's* watery grave; Rear Admiral Richard E. Byrd, the first aviator to fly over the South Pole; and Captain Nathaniel B. Palmer, who accidentally discovered Antarctica.

Now was the time for me to join their ranks, to start living life on the edge. Maybe I could become thin and famous like Amelia Earhart. Like her, I am fairly tall, my middle initial is M, I have a gap between my two front teeth, and until I looked it up, I couldn't spell medieval either (more on that and her wedding day later). Unlike Amelia, I wasn't skinny, but that was about to change. I would stop lying around reading about adventurers and do what it took to become one.

My husband, Jim, and I were transferred to the Mystic area by his company, which meant I had to quit my job as a full-time writer for a college and search for a new one in a community revolving around life at sea—not easy for a confirmed desk sitter like me. Finding the area already teeming with underemployed writers and publicists, I was grateful when my former employer hired me back as a consulting writer. Although freelancing allowed me to work from home in my pajamas, it offered no retirement benefits—hence the need to become famous. Being famous not only helps pay the bills, but it gives you an edge when trying to accomplish other goals.

Now was the time for me to follow in the path of prominent authors such as Herman Melville who went to sea on a whaler (a ship designed to catch whales and process their oil) when he couldn't find a job. Although he deserted and had to live among cannibals for a time, he found the inspiration to write his first novel. Further sea adventures, which included mutiny and learning about a whale that rammed and sank the *Essex*, led to the creation of his magnum opus: *Moby Dick*. I, myself, could barely get through this "Great American Novel," but somebody must like it. And now that I lived within walking distance of the *Charles W. Morgan*, the last wooden whaleship in the world, I wondered if that was a sign. Perhaps I could enlist on it as a deck swabber on some epic voyage. The house we purchased came with a brass, whale-shaped door knocker. Now that had to be a sign.

If following in the footsteps of a whaling writer didn't work, there was always the chance I could get famous by finding a dead body—just like Bailey and our older daughter had. Although it didn't make her into an international celebrity, I use it as a party stopper whenever I want to be the center of attention. Of course, I should really find my own body, preferably of a well-known person. Celebrities are always coming to Mystic to film movies or vacation.

Since I couldn't count on finding a dead body, famous or otherwise, I decided to start small. First, I planned to compile "The 7 Wonders of Mystic"—something quick I could shout to the tourists who rolled down their car windows asking what they should see (besides my underwear).

National Geographic's website suggests that Mystic adventurers bike what it calls the 25-mile Vineyard Loop that includes "some hairy climbs that stops at two of the best wineries." Hairy climbs? I hoped to get thin, but did I have to go uphill to do it? I thought not.

Instead, I would conquer a trail of my own design—one that would avoid hills where possible—and call it the "Mystic Seafarer's Trail." It would include "The 7 Wonders" (once I figured out what they were), plus the stomping grounds of legendary explorers. It would encompass the Mystic, Stonington and Noank area and even include where Kate the acupuncturist weighed her newborn on a lobster scale after giving birth on a schooner and rowing to shore.

With so many potential wonders to consider and adventures to try, I had a lot of ground—and water—to cover. So, every afternoon, I checked my skirt and off Bailey and I went to follow a scent of our own.

2 THE HAUNTS AND HOUNDS OF MYSTICVILLE

With no friends in Mystic yet, I was grateful to have Bailey as my side-kick in my search for "The 7 Wonders" and an epic adventure. Together, we traversed the winding, narrow streets lined with 19th century homes, wrought iron fences, and hitching posts for horses.

Many homes display hand-painted plaques stating year built, first owners and their occupations. Some long-ago residents were blacksmiths and merchants, but many were sea captains and ship builders—several during the California Gold Rush era. Although more people died of scurvy than found gold, ship builders and sea captains could make a lot of money transporting prospectors and supplies to California. Some minors traded gold for potatoes, ounce for ounce, because potatoes were known to combat scurvy (potatoes contain vitamin C).[ii]

Between reading plaques and meeting my neighbors, it became overwhelmingly obvious: Mystic was stuffed with adventurers—living and dead. I particularly liked the dead ones because they wouldn't complain if I wrote about them.

Unlike the living, those who have gone to the Great Beyond remain blissfully quiet and let me tell their story the best way I see fit. When I published the private love letters of my great-great grandparents in my book, *Ever True: A Union Private and His Wife*, I didn't hear a peep out of them—despite the secrets they revealed.

Because Amelia Earhart had simply disappeared, she couldn't complain when writers came up with all sorts of scenarios for her final moments. In addition to her crashing into the Pacific Ocean after failing to find Howland Island, there was the theory she was captured and executed by the Japanese as a spy. One book suggested she was alive and residing in New Jersey under a different identity.[iii] (Why she would hide there is beyond me. Is there something really bad about being thin and famous I should know

4

about?)

In an effort to keep the living happy about my "7 Wonders of Mystic" project and minimize their complaints when my choices were published, I introduced my quest with a well-defined set of criteria—such as the wonder must be located in the actual village of Mystic and still exist (residents had wanted me to write about a large, controversial statue even though it had been moved to another part of Connecticut). With the help of the Greater Mystic Chamber of Commerce, who would publish the results on their website, I came up with the following criteria. All wonders had to be:

- A "wow" site, provoking a second look
- Open year-round
- Free to view from the outside
- Within Mystic's zip code (06355)

With criteria in hand, my daily wonder-seeking routine began precisely at noon so Bailey and I could stroll downtown to the bell chimes of a massive New England-style church perched precariously on the edge of a little cliff near my house. Overseeing the Mystic Valley, the former Mariner's Free Church doubled in size when a team of oxen dragged another church building up the hill on sleds in 1861 to unite the two buildings—well in time to accommodate the 1,000 residents who gathered to mourn Abraham Lincoln after his assassination. Now called the Union Baptist Church, its original steeple was destroyed in the Hurricane of 1938 and rebuilt even taller in 1969. Visible and heard throughout the valley, it was an overwhelming presence. Should it be declared a Mystic Wonder?

Another site to consider was the large, eight-sided house several doors down the street from mine on West Mystic Avenue. The octagon house was built in 1850, two years after an American doctor published a book declaring that octagon shaped homes were healthier to live in. Although a private home (ironically, its house address is number 8), some Mystic locals have gotten a tour. Inside stairs wrap around in sets of eight, with notches cut at each turn to accommodate the carrying of a coffin. With its dome-shaped, glass cupola on its roof restored after the Hurricane of 1938, it is one of the few of its kind left in the country. That makes it an official Mystic Wonder, doesn't it?

I mustn't be too hasty—there could only be seven wonders, and I had already seen several intriguing sites—many passionately loved by the locals who knew and loved the history behind them. Yet a tourist just passing through wouldn't know the history—and most wouldn't care. I had to remember one of my criteria—it needed to be a site that provoked a second look, whether one knew its secrets or not.

Luckily for me, Bailey was a big help in meeting people. Pedestrians, curious about his confusing breed and woe-be-gone expression, often approached to ask, "What kind of dog is he?" or "He looks so sad—can I pet him?" Tourists, especially those from other countries who missed their own dogs, actually kissed him on the face in hopes of cheering him up. I didn't spoil the moment by revealing his fondness for rolling around in dead fish.

Bailey loved the attention and knew which way to walk to get it. It didn't take him long to pick his own set of wonders. No, not the octagon house, or the Greek Revival homes along the Mystic River known as "Captain's Row." Bailey had no interest in trotting past the house where the ghost of a harmless, old woman is said to reside; nor the one belonging to the captain of the *Andrew Jackson*, the famous Mystic-built clipper that made the record-breaking run from New York to San Francisco in 89 days and 4 hours in 1860; nor to the one where coffins were built in the basement.[iv]

No, first and foremost, Bailey wanted to trot toward the Green Marble Coffee House. There, he might get a special nose greeting from Otto, the golden retriever purchased at half price because his tail broke off at birth. Often escaping from his home near Captain's Row, Otto stopped at the crosswalk on West Main Street before trotting to the other side. Then he would head toward Peacock Alley, where patrons of the Green Marble, including his master, gathered to play music or just hang out.

Bailey also loved seeing what was new at the Mystic pet shop, Stonington Feeds. It was there that co-owner Genevieve introduced him to his favorite treat in the world—bovine trachea. Seeing the repulsed look on my face when she first showed it to Bailey and me, Genevieve said, "Oh, don't worry, we only sell organically fed bovine body parts." That's not exactly what was "worrying" me. Bailey also loves her cow hooves, but has yet to try the duck feet. Some things I just don't want to see lying around my living room floor. Peaches, the resident cockatoo, can't stand when Genevieve shows Bailey around and screeches to become the center of attention again. The moment Bailey spots Genevieve's 18-year-old cat, Old Lady Kitty, stretching lazily over the large bags of organic dog kibble, it's time to leave.

Despite Bailey's wonder preferences, and those of the locals, I finally narrowed Mystic's intriguing sights down to seven wonders (no, bovine trachea isn't among them). When "The 7 Wonders of Mystic" was published on the Greater Mystic Chamber of Commerce's website, some of my wonder choices earned the respect of the locals—if they agreed with me. Others did not.

Much to the disapproval of Mystic residents, the "open year-round" criteria meant that Clyde's Cider Mill, the oldest steam powered cider mill in the United States, could not be included because it's only open in the fall.

The Mystic zip code requirement also knocked out some of my own personal favorites such as the hidden tunnel at Fort Griswold in Groton (the site of the massacre of patriots by British troops under the command of traitor Benedict Arnold), and the *Nautilus*, the world's first nuclear powered submarine and first vessel to complete an undersea voyage to the North Pole in 1958.

Other "wow" sites that could not be included were the "Emerald City" exterior of Foxwoods, the largest casino in the northeast, and the massive, glass Casino of the Sky at Mohegan Sun. They are located on nearby Indian reservations, but not directly in Mystic.

Fortunately for tourists, many who come by train from New York City and Boston, the Mystic zip code criteria means that all wonders are within a two-mile walk or bike ride from the Mystic Train Depot. Tourists and locals can borrow bicycles for free (Mystic Community Bikes, a nonprofit organization, likes to call their hospitality "bike sharing"), to get to each one. Those who travel by bus to Olde Mistick Village (yes, that's how the colonial style shopping center is spelled), can also find free bicycles to "share." In fact, there are several locations where a bike can be borrowed.[v]

Not only can energetic souls ride past each wonder and wonder contender, they can continue on to reach all the points of interest I discovered and placed on the Mystic Seafarer's Trail, which stretches a little beyond the Mystic zip code area into Stonington, Noank and Groton.

Some of the "7 Wonders of Mystic" inspire folks to plan an adventure around what they represent, yet all please relaxing tourists who just want to look at them without having to do anything about them.

Each and every wonder, however, did inspire me to action—giving me hope that an epic adventure was just around the corner. The next seven chapters are broken up into two parts. The first part gives you the wonder and the secrets behind it. The second part describes the adventure—or rather misadventure—it launched.

3 WONDER #1: WHALESHIP, CHARLES W. MORGAN

Although the majority of the country's wooden ships built in the mid-1800s are gone, some are enjoying their retirement years in Mystic. One in particular is not only history-making, but a sight to behold—especially now that it has been hauled out of the water. Seen towering above the homes lining the Mystic River, on the corner of Isham and Bay Streets, without any argument from the locals, is the first official Mystic Wonder—the *Charles W. Morgan*—the last wooden whaleship in the world.

Even Governor Dannel P. Malloy loves the *Morgan* and designated the 2013-2014 academic year to be the "Year of the Charles W. Morgan" in the State of Connecticut.

Looking very much like someone heard it's time to build another ark, the *Charles W. Morgan* is presently undergoing restoration at Mystic Seaport. In its long career, the *Morgan* witnessed floggings, stowaways, drownings, desertions, amputations, burials at sea, and men who took the "Nantucket sleigh ride"—a high-speed whaleboat ride sometimes given by a harpooned whale.

If one touches the *Morgan*, launched during the height of the whaling industry in 1841, one is not only touching a vessel that has survived typhoons, hurricanes, crushing ice, stirrings of a mutiny, and an attack by Pacific Islanders, one is also touching a movie star. Featured in several films, including Steven Spielberg's *Amistad* with actor Morgan Freeman, the *Charles W. Morgan* can be viewed in her (a ship is still referred to as "she" even if it has a male name) original role as a whaling ship in a 1922 film playing inside Mystic Seaport.

Visitors to the *Morgan* will not only see the industry side of whaling, like the brick furnace used to process the blubber into oil, but they will also see the personal side, such as the captain's cabin that includes a private "head" (toilet to the sea), sitting room, and a gimbal (always level)

8

bed installed by a captain so his wife could sleep comfortably despite the pitch of the sea.

When actor William Hurt climbed aboard the *Morgan* to prepare for his role as Captain Ahab in the TV mini-series *Moby Dick*, he sat on a sailor's bunk with Mystic Seaport staff members and talked for an hour about what life aboard a whaleship must have been like. "This is the only place in the world where he could have done that," said Matthew Stackpole, the ship's historian.

The *Morgan* arrived at Mystic Seaport, a 19-acre maritime museum, in 1941. Having been in a derelict condition for several years, Mystic Seaport's shipwrights got her back into shape. Since then, approximately 20 million visitors have crossed her decks.

Kick-off to Adventure:
How to Boat "Mystic Style"

The *Morgan*, like many of the vessels residing in Mystic, is a constant reminder of the one sure-fire way to find adventure in Mystic—by sailing out of it. The *Morgan* is scheduled to take to the high seas again in 2014. But this time, whales will be safe because she is going out as an educational vessel. If I'm not needed as a deck swabber or some other low-skill sailing job, perhaps I could sneak on as a stow-away. Now that would give me a chance to write the next *Moby Dick*!

First, I needed to do my homework on the whaling industry in general, and on the *Morgan* specifically. Once a year, the public is invited to remain onboard overnight for a 24-hour marathon reading of *Moby Dick*. In a desperate attempt to get through that wordy book, I reserved my spot on deck. Although I slept through most of the nighttime reading (except when I snuck outside to grab the free brownies stationed nearby), some of the book sank in, giving me insights on life aboard a whaler. When a particularly dramatic volunteer reader yelled Melville's words, "Man overboard!", a fast asleep career Navy man abruptly stopped snoring, opened his eyes in alarm, and yelled from his sleeping bag, "Man overboard!"

Reaching his ear as quickly as I could, I whispered, "It's just part of the story; go back to sleep."

When I teased him about his outburst the following morning, he said, "Well, 'man overboard' is a call to action at sea."

Even if I never got to set sail on the *Morgan* or yell "man overboard," one thing was for certain—I just had to learn how to tie sailor's knots and discuss tides if I ever wanted to fit in with this community.

I was shocked upon moving to Mystic to learn how unfair tides are—their highs and lows don't occur at the same time every day. In addition, low tide isn't always the same low and high tide isn't always the same high—it all depends on the phase of the moon that day. A tide is at its highest at full moon. I thought grade school teachers just made that stuff up.

No wonder I overheard community members ask each other about tides all the time. Sailors and fishermen based their entire day around them. When a fisherman said I could go along with him on his rounds to see what his day was like, I asked what time I should meet him at his boat the following Wednesday.

He replied, "At high tide."

Huh? How was I supposed to know when that was? "Can't you just give me a time?" I asked.

He explained there were charts giving those times—he just didn't know off-hand. Each area has their own tide chart—one chart does not fit all. So much to learn about maritime life! For example, there are two high and low tides a day, in addition to slack tides, where nothing interesting happens at all. (I have since uploaded "tideApp" to my phone to get daily information on height and times of low and high tide, sunset, moonset, etc., for Noank, Connecticut, which is at the mouth of Mystic River.)

To begin my boating education, Jim agreed to join me in purchasing passage aboard some of the Mystic area vessels, which included a steamboat, a schooner, and a re-outfitted lobster boat.

Unbelievably, I found the hardest part of boating is knowing what to bring. It's not as easy as you think—especially since there seems to be an unwritten "Boating Mystic-Style" code. I had to learn the hard way.

Our first boat ride was on the *Sabino*, the oldest coal-fired steamboat still in operation in the United States. Built in 1908, it's owned and operated by Mystic Seaport and is one of the few National Historic Landmarks you can actually ride on (the cable cars in San Francisco are another). While chugging down the Mystic River, you can watch coal being shoveled into a hot boiler that keeps her going.

Our trip on the *Sabino* was a Saturday night, 90-minute excursion. I realized my first mistake the moment we boarded—I should have brought a full-fledged picnic to enjoy the trip "Mystic-style." I looked on in envy as passengers took out bottles of wine, plastic cups, cheese, crackers, and all sorts of culinary delights from their wicker baskets. And there Jim and I sat, with a lousy jar of almonds and some bottled water I pulled from my ratty, old knapsack.

When we booked another evening sail on the tall schooner *Argia*, I vowed things would be different—this time, we would bring elegant snacks and drinks. I packed a bottle of wine in addition to almonds and bottled water. I even thought to bring pretty, blue plastic cups in keeping with the color of the waters we were about to sail.

Well, I knew right away we underpacked when I saw a party of six adults pull out real wine glasses with their bottles of wine. Suddenly, my blue plastic cups seemed so cheesy—so inadequate on this tall, seaworthy sailboat. And when the adults broke out a tray of shrimp cocktail from their large, Mary Poppins-style picnic bag, that was too much. I tried making friendly conversation with them so they'd share their shrimp, but they didn't warm to my advances. Another family with young children also had the better of us. I couldn't help but be envious when they lifted one cheesy pizza slice after another from their Mystic Pizza take-out boxes. They didn't share with us either. I thought of the tasty, thin crust pizza from Pizzetta—a place we frequented often to enjoy the outdoor seating and view of Mystic River. Why hadn't I thought to take a pie from there to go?

Thankfully, the *Argia* provided cheese, crackers and fruit, so I ate a lot of that and loudly declared things like, "Yummy!" so the others would think I preferred the *Argia's* food to theirs.

My other mistake was that I was underdressed—it got very cold that foggy evening on the Mystic River and the Sound. The *Argia* did, however, provide blankets. The males on the voyage were too macho to wrap one around themselves, so they shivered like real men or went below deck.

In March, we took a seal watch cruise on a re-outfitted offshore lobster boat with Project Oceanology, which departed from nearby Groton. This time I vowed to stay warm, but *again* we didn't wear the right clothes. I should have worn foul-weather gear (shiny, waterproof yellow pants and jacket), instead of jeans and a down, winter jacket. Our jeans got wet and froze to our legs. Although we were warned this would happen if we stood on the bow where we would hit every wave head-on, who wants to sit inside or stand on the stern (back of the boat)? Well, eventually we did.

At least my feet stayed dry because I wore my thick, water-proof shoes. But poor Jim—he wore leather shoes, making me think of the stow-a-way sailor on Earnest Shackleton's trans-Antarctic expedition who had his toes amputated because they froze solid in his leather boots.

Although we did spot more than 200 harbor seals, they didn't do much—just lay around on rocks in what's known as a "banana" pose to keep their heads and tails out of the water. Unlike sea lions, they are shaped like blobs and don't do fancy tricks. The big excitement for me, much bigger than watching lazy seals take up rock space, was the reporter who came along with her video camera. While the other passengers were busy making the most of the voyage, either by recording the number of seals we saw along with the location, time and temperature; giggling with their binoculars on an all-girl birthday party; or simply sitting around fighting sea sickness; I kept busy trying to catch the reporter's eye so she'd feature me in her news clip. I figured you never know—some director might see it and say, "Hey, watch that middle-aged woman study those lazy seals—she'd make a great leading lady in our next epic seagoing movie for baby boomers!"

Despite my attention-getting efforts, the reporter filmed all around me to catch the do-nothing seals and the giggling birthday party girls. But Jim made it into the published news clip—I caught a glimpse of him with his binoculars standing behind the party of girls.[vi] (Note to self: next time I'm in public, carry a prop such as binoculars, wear a weird, eye-catching hat, or station myself next to kids.)

Returning back to Mystic after our seal watch, we dried off in front of the large, stone fireplace in the lower level pub area of the Captain Daniel Packer Inne—the very place the *National Geographic* website said we would feel like a character in *Moby Dick*. The Inne was built more than 250 years ago in 1758 by Captain Daniel Packer who operated a ferry across Mystic River. Packer liked to entertain his guests, mostly travelers between New York and Boston, with tales of his high sea adventures.[vii]

Although there were some similarities in the maritime décor of the Captain Daniel Packer Inne and the Spouter-Inn of *Moby Dick* (minus the clubs and spears "tufted with knots of human hair"), the Packer Inne was much more comfortable. The Spouter-Inn, for example, didn't have their fire going when sailor Ishmael entered. Herman Melville wrote: *"It was cold as Iceland—no fire at all—the landlord said he couldn't afford it...We were fain to button up our monkey jackets, and hold to our lips cups of scalding tea with our half frozen fingers."*

Unlike Ishmael, we didn't meet any shrunken head dealers or whalers with beards "stiff with icicles," but we did enjoy squeezing next to a female prison guard at a tiny table beside the fireplace. Without a ship to sail, she didn't try to persuade us to serve as crew on some grueling voyage, but she did regale us with fun prison escape stories—like the time a woman dressed in an orange prison outfit asked a convenience store owner for change to make a phone call—which ultimately led to her recapture.

As we warmed ourselves beside the fire drinking red wine and dipping sweet potato fries into a raspberry sauce, I tried to regale the prison guard back with our seal watching saga, complete with vivid details of the rough seas and cold spray. She wasn't impressed—especially since Jim kept interrupting my story to say the seas weren't that rough and our wet jeans weren't really "stiff with icicles." (Note to self: never recount my adventures with Jim around.)

One thing became very clear to me that day. To have a truly gripping story, one that could launch a *New York Times* bestseller, I would have to allow myself to get shanghaied into serving as crew on a very long, hazardous voyage. Other Mystic residents were forced to serve as seamen against their will. Prior to the War of 1812, the British were fond of seizing Americans off shore to serve in the Royal Navy (called impressment).

Yet Mystic itself became a place where raiders and smugglers could hide from the British. I probably never would have been pressed into involuntary service while sitting at the Daniel Packer Inne. Well, at least not during the War of 1812. Just above us was a rock ledge that was once the site of Fort Rachel.

The British referred to the lower Mystic River as a "hornet's nest" because the locals harassed their blockading ships and attacked them repeatedly under sail, from small boats, and even from Fort Rachel itself. (According to area folklore, Fort Rachel was named after the woman who lived below it because she provided comfort to the men—and I don't just mean food and water.)

Now that the British no longer needed to be afraid to venture up the Mystic River, perhaps I would meet a sea captain looking for help sailing a vessel back to England. Better yet would be to find a friend in Mystic with a boat—one who would be happy to cart me around on some epic voyage and give me a shot at fame and fortune.

4   WONDER #2: MYSTIC AQUARIUM'S "CROWNS" (HOME OF *TITANIC* EXHIBIT)

Strolling through Olde Mistick Village, you will feel like a time traveler as you drink from the old-fashioned water pump and nibble on homemade fudge from Franklin's General Store. Once you near the parking lot, however, you will be cast into another world by the sight of a massive, blue King Neptune-like crown rising out of it.

What you are seeing is the outside structure of Mystic Aquarium's Ocean Exploration Center, where the discoverer of the grave of the *R.M.S. Titanic*, Dr. Robert Ballard, keeps his home office and exhibit.

My reaction to this nautical sighting is exactly what famed international architect Cesar Pelli was going for. He designed some of the world's most recognizable structures, including Canary Wharf Tower in London, Britain's tallest building.

The Ocean Exploration Center, which features *"Titanic* – 12,450 Feet Below," is part of Mystic Aquarium, where Pelli also designed the glass entryway canopy. Reminiscent of the Statue of Liberty's crown, it's called the Ocean Planet Pavilion. Pelli's goal was to transform the visitor into an explorer. He states: "In this aquarium, the visitors have entered a new environment—they have left behind our known world."

Explorers do not cross under the glass canopy to enter this "unknown world" alone. Welcoming one in are seagulls perched on the canopy tips and smaller birds flitting among the rafters above. Erin Merz of Mystic Aquarium, said, "We happily invite birds to nest in the Ocean Planet Pavilion. Most of them are sparrows."

Inside the aquarium, sea lions perform, fish swim, and seals scoot along on rocks as best they can with their awkwardly shaped bodies. In one quiet corner, I peered through windows to glimpse a rescued seal receiving medical attention before being released back into the wild.

The beluga whales provide more face-to-face interaction. They were just as curious about me as I was of them as we watched each other through the glass of one of the largest beluga whale habitats in the nation. One whale became particularly interested in the guide dog standing nearby and pressed its blubbery head into the glass to get a closer look. The dog, unafraid of most obstacles in her way, drew back in concern—she had not been trained to negotiate around a whale.

For those interested in visiting the grave of the *Titanic* through their imagination, explorers can stroll through the state-of-the-art exhibit, "*Titanic* – 12,450 Feet Below," where Dr. Ballard shares his discovery of the famous, "unsinkable" ship. He states, "I grew up wanting to be Captain Nemo from Jules Verne's 20,000 Leagues Under the Sea." Well, he's done it.

Dr. Ballard is now able to reveal the secret mission behind his search for the *Titanic*. Only in 2008 had it been declassified by the U.S. Navy, allowing him to do so. Excerpt from the Mystic Aquarium website:

"As a commanding officer in the Naval Reserve, Dr. Ballard turned to the U. S. Navy for financial support to test his invention, the ARGO-Jason, a remotely operated vehicle (ROV) system to locate and videotape underwater objects. In the summer of 1985, in exchange for funds and time to look for Titanic, he was commissioned with a secret mission to explore two Navy nuclear submarines that went down in the 1960s in search of their nuclear reactors and weapons systems, one off the coast of Massachusetts, the other in the Azores.

"With the ARGO proving successful and mission accomplished, Dr. Ballard sped to the Grand Banks to search for Titanic. Though he had only 12 days to find the ship, Dr. Ballard had made an important discovery while documenting the two submarines—in both cases the downed subs left a long debris trail. Dr. Ballard calculated that if he could find Titanic's debris trail, it would lead him to the ship.

"Narrowing his search to 50 square miles, he ordered ARGO to make sweeps one mile apart. Nine days flew by and hopes were dimming. Then, at 12:48 a.m. on September 1, 1985, ARGO's operator spotted debris. Dr. Ballard raced to the control room and entered just as ARGO glided over one of Titanic's 29 boilers..."[viii]

What struck Dr. Ballard the most when he viewed the wreckage of the *Titanic* were the pairs of shoes lying together on the ocean bottom. Shoes were all that could be found of the victims. The sight affected him so much, he made sure to include a reconstruction of them on the sea floor in his exhibit.

The plaque on the shoe exhibit explains that sea creatures and a "*deep water environment unsaturated in calcium carbonate dissolve the skeleton, leaving only leather shoes behind. Treated with tannic acid in manufacturing, the leather shoes endure as a memorial to those men, women and children who went down with the ship."*

Of the 2,200 passengers and crew who left Southampton, England, on the *Titanic* on April 10, 1912, only 700 survived. Of the 1,500 who died, only 337 bodies were recovered--and not all of those could be identified.

Shipwrecks and Shoes

Now that I lived close to the rocky waters off New England, with an underwater terrain that causes countless shipwrecks, was it possible for me to find a one?

One area resident, the owner of Cottrell Brewing Co., recently discovered the shipwreck of *USS Revenge*, a ship commanded by U.S. Navy hero Capt. Oliver Hazard Perry who lost the ship when it struck Watch Hill Reef in 1811. Located in waters off nearby Watch Hill in Rhode Island, the discovery made Charles Cottrell Buffum Jr., a scuba diver when not making beer, and his diving partner, Craig Harger, into celebrities. Buffum has since released a beer called Perry's Revenge Ale.

When I asked Buffum about the possibility of others finding shipwrecks in the area, he said a good place to start looking is in the book, *Shipwrecks on the Shores of Westerly*, by Margaret Carter, which lists over 230 recorded wrecks between 1671 and 1963 in the Westerly-Stonington-Fishers Island area. Buffum said, "And this is considered only a partial list! This is no surprise, given all of the rocks, reefs and shoals out there. And even today, with our sophisticated GPS and radar technologies, boats and ships continue to wreck on these obstructions. I have personally witnessed two while diving out there. So there is never a shortage of wrecks to look for." [ix]

Amelia Earhart, like everyone else, was interested in shipwrecks, or at least in the *Titanic* tragedy. While held up in Newfoundland waiting for favorable weather before taking off with her fellow aviators on her first flight across the Atlantic in 1928, she read *The Story of the Titanic Disaster*.[x] She would have been amazed at the technical advances that made it possible to locate the *Titanic* 73 years after its sinking. Will similar advances make it possible to find the remains of her plane, missing now for 75 years? If so, will her shoes—her final resting place—be found? Since I still hadn't found a friend with a boat, I wasn't likely to be the one to find Amelia's shoes. But was it possible for me to find the owner of a pair of the *Titanic's* shoes?

One brown pair of leather shoes lying together in the *Titanic* shoe exhibit obviously belonged to a man. Could they have belonged to the young newlywed Lucian Philip Smith, who insisted his teenage bride get in the lifeboat? They had gotten married on February 7, 1912. A little more than two months later, on April 14, the *Titanic* struck an iceberg.

I became interested in this couple in 2006 when assigned to write about Manhattan's Chelsea district by a real estate developer. In addition to researching the trendy shops, art galleries and restaurants of Chelsea, I found myself traveling back in time through an old *New York Times* article dated April 19, 1912, about a historic event that occurred in Chelsea the previous evening on Pier 54:

"Rescue Ship Arrives—Thousands Gather At the Pier."

I imagined myself crowding with the others on the evening of April 18th to catch the first sight of *Titanic* survivors disembarking from the *Carpathia* on Pier 54. I could especially picture this one distraught woman, still in her teens, who ran to her father's waiting arms: *"Mrs. Lucian B. Smith, the bride of a few weeks, who was forced to sit helpless in a lifeboat while she watched the Titanic carry her husband to his death, was one of the first off the ship. Her father, Congressman Hughes of Virginia, was waiting for her. Her eyes swept the crowd for a glimpse of him and they sighted each other at the same moment. Girl and man rushed toward each other, the crowd separating that they might meet, and Mrs. Smith, with a cry, fell fainting into her father's arms."*

Mrs. Smith (maiden name Mary Eloise Hughes) was only 18 when she and her husband, Lucian Philip Smith, boarded the *Titanic* on Wednesday, April 10, 1912, to return home from their European honeymoon. She was asleep in their first class stateroom the following Sunday evening, April 14th, while her husband played cards in the Café Parisien. At 20 minutes before midnight, the *Titanic* struck an iceberg. Mr. Smith rushed to the stateroom to awaken her.

The couple reached the deck when the third lifeboat, which contained the pregnant Mrs. John Jacob Astor, was being lowered. Although Mary clung to Lucian, he insisted she get into the boat. That act not only saved Mary, but his unborn child—one he may not have known even existed. Approximately eight months after the sinking, Mary gave birth to their son, Lucian P. Smith II. [xi]

I just had to see the spot where Mrs. Smith fainted into her father's arms on the night of April 18, 1912. Now a somewhat isolated spot in New York City, I felt the ghosts of the past as Jim and I crossed under an archway faintly marked, "White Star and Cunard," and onto Pier 54. Unlike that busy, terrible night nearly 100 years earlier, the pier had an eerie, lonely feeling. Yet the evening the survivors returned, the *New York Times* article reported that the pier *"echoed with the shrieks of women and even men, who seemed driven temporarily insane by their experiences of the last few days."*

Mr. Lucian P. Smith's body was never recovered, or if it was, it was never positively identified. Could that reproduction of shoes lying on the ocean floor in Mystic's *Titanic* exhibit be replicating his final resting place?

5 WONDER #3: THE HANGING GARDENS

Out of a widow's loneliness sprang a stone landscape so intriguing, it should be referred to as the "Hanging Gardens" of Enders Island. But you must stroll through slowly if you hope to appreciate the absurdity of a brass bird spigot beside a cat statue, or the whimsy of a heart-shaped stone path.

The driving force behind this maze of rock hedges and archways was Alys E. Enders, widow of Dr. Thomas B. Enders. Having outlived Thomas by many years, Alys found a way to ensure companionship on her 11-acre island estate.

"She was always adding on to her mansion and gardens just to keep the workers from leaving the grounds." says Jeffrey Anderson, Executive Director of St. Edmunds Retreat, the Catholic oasis that now occupies the island. Alys donated her estate to the Catholic Church upon her death in 1954.

Worried you might not be welcome—especially if you're not Catholic? The website declares, "Not a Catholic? Not a problem…all are welcomed to enjoy the peaceful natural beauty of our island."

And peace you will surely find as you listen to the waves of Fishers Island Sound slap against the rocky shore and stroll past tiled pools, fountains, and Alys' former tea house, now the three-sided Seaside Chapel that protects an altar covered with hand-written prayers (some very personal and heart wrenching), funeral cards of missed loved ones, and unlit cigarettes cast off by repentant smokers. On the concrete floor are Alys' initials, A.E.E., presumably engraved by her in 1951.

The island's mansion and chapel, which displays relics (including the actual withered arm of Saint Edmund who preached for the Sixth Crusade in 1228), are used for twelve step recovery programs, retreats, sacred art workshops and daily mass. Jams and jellies (with names like "Fire and Brimstone" Hot Pepper Jelly), are made from fruit grown on the island and are available for sale.

How to Make Friends in Mystic

I thought about poor Alys and her loneliness in Mystic. Like her, I too hired a handyman—really my first friend in Mystic. Thinking I only needed his help with the odds and ends of moving into a new home, he realized that if I was ever going to make friends, he needed to help me better assimilate in my community. He worried that I would end up lonely like Alys if I didn't make our home more seaworthy in keeping with the Mystic culture.

So, in addition to hanging our window shades, he took it upon himself to help me decorate. A long-time resident and boat-owner, he encouraged me to dig through my boxes and pull out any maritime knick-knacks I could find. Thinking I was nautical enough with my whale door knocker, he prodded me along to do better than that. So, with much effort, I finally found stuff I hadn't displayed in years, such as cheap ship models picked up from tourist shops, and pieces of driftwood and shells collected on beach vacations.

When it came time to hang paintings, he scowled at my watercolor of a frozen lake surrounded by mountains. I wanted it placed over our fireplace, the place of honor, because it reminded me of Harriman State Park, near our former home in New York (where Bailey and our older daughter found the dead body). Instead, my handyman favored our watercolor of boats moored to a dock. He said, "You live in Mystic now. You should put this painting over the fireplace." Terrified of feeling Alys' loneliness on Enders Island, I did as I was told. Perhaps that boat painting would entice a boat owner to go from being my acquaintance to being my friend—the kind that would offer me a chance at an epic sea voyage.

Unlike Alys, I couldn't afford to keep hiring people to come over to keep me company (unless, of course, I met my goal of becoming famous) so I decided to throw a last-minute Memorial Day party and invite everyone I'd met so far—from my handyman and his wife, to all my new neighbors.

None of our neighbors came. Were they still recovering from my "wardrobe malfunction" debut? Was that why they shooed their children indoors whenever Bailey and I walked by?

Although many said they had previous plans, we were able to rustle up some folks happy not to host their own Memorial Day shindig, such as strangers I'd met on the street walking Bailey and Jim's co-workers, Gene and Fran, who had never met me (or my wardrobe). I didn't have to worry about being nautical to fit in with Gene and Fran—they could care less about tide charts and sailor's knots. Being reptile lovers and reptile convention attenders, however, they just wanted to know why Jim and I didn't want a lizard or a snake. They weren't impressed by Bailey at all.

Bailey did have one fan in attendance at the party—Bambi (yes that is her real name). In fact, Bailey is probably the main reason she considered getting to know me. We met at the Department of Motor Vehicles in Old Saybrook (where Katharine Hepburn lived) when I applied for my Connecticut driver's license.

Spending hours there together in typical DMV-style, I learned that Bambi owned several rescue cats, dogs, rabbits, a horse and a bearded dragon (lizard). When she learned that I was the third owner of a beagle/basset hound mix who was waiting impatiently for me at home, she asked for my card. Did she assume I was heroic like her and airlifted Bailey out of some dangerous situation? All we did was rescue him from a household of four cats who had little use for a hound who chased them around all day.

Expecting never to hear from Bambi again when I revealed I was just a lady who wanted a free dog, I was surprised when she called me that very afternoon. She said, "I just got home and plan to spend the afternoon beside my pool with my dogs, one of which is my basset hound Edgar. I'd love to meet Bailey to see what Edgar would look like if he had some beagle in him."

While her inside pets were being chased around by Rumba, a robotic vacuum cleaner, Bambi and I lounged beside her pool with our hounds and discussed life in Mystic. Sounding very much like a "Hallmark movie,"[xii] she told me all about its annual traditions—how Santa comes up the Mystic River by tugboat to kick off Christmas and the lighted boat parade, and how the whole community comes out for the Downtown Mystic Holiday Stroll, which includes free cookies in shops and carolers in top hats.

In February, locals take a break from winter at the Cabin Fever Festival & Charity Chowder Cook at Olde Mistick Village. When summer comes, there are endless celebrations such as the antique boat parade, free concerts and movies at Mystic River Park, and Mystic Seaport's annual dog parade, where Edgar and Bailey had a shot at becoming Sea Dog of the Week.

As I learned about my new community, our hounds became fast friends. Engaging in acts unfit to print, Edgar, who insists on wearing his green argyle sweater most of the year, probably reasoned that since Bailey was half basset hound, they must be "kissing cousins." At any rate, Bailey made a new friend—and so did I.

6   WONDER #4: MYSTIC RIVER DRAWBRIDGE

Images of the Mystic drawbridge, which is considered a local icon, are featured on everything from mugs to t-shirts and the locally brewed beer, Mystic Bridge IPA.

If you are strolling across the bridge licking your ice-cream cone while taking in views of the tall ships along the Mystic River, and suddenly have ringing in your ears, don't be alarmed—everyone else is hearing it too. But you must quickly get to the other side because the bridge is about to lift.

Once the bridge operator, who is watching you from a little house perched above, sees that you are safely to one side, he will pull the whistle cord signaling to the mariners on the river below that the bridge is ready to rise.

Watching the historic 1922 drawbridge, called a bascule bridge because of its seesaw design, lifted by the massive, overhead concrete counterweights is thrilling to pedestrians as well as to the bridge operators, called tenders, who man the bridge house 24 hours a day (yes, there is a bathroom).

Bridge tender Bruce Sullivan, known around Mystic as "Sully," said, "I have the best view to watch all kinds of vessels go through—schooners, clippers, sloops, tugboats." He was particularly excited to watch the maiden voyage of the *Amistad* replica, built at Mystic Seaport. "I've seen the yachts of Steven Spielberg, Clint Eastwood and Phil Donahue." How does he know those were celebrity yachts? "Because [those celebrities] stood on their decks and waved up to me!"

This National Historic Landmark is itself a celebrity and was prominently featured in the movie, *Mystic Pizza*. Sully got to meet Julia Roberts during the filming in 1987.

Bridge tender Rod Coleman was especially excited to meet former President Jimmy Carter who shook his hand and personally thanked him for keeping the bridge down during the tightly-timed schedule created by the Secret Service for Carter's motorcade. Carter and former first lady Rosalynn were staying in Mystic for the 2004 christening of the Navy submarine, *Jimmy Carter*, in nearby Groton.

Located on U.S. Route 1, the Mystic River drawbridge replaced a steel swing bridge. A prior wooden bridge used oxen to move the span and another version of the bridge posted the sign, "WALK YOUR HORSES," to keep vibrations to a minimum. Before the first bridge was built in 1819, people crossed the river by ferry.

As thrilling as it is for pedestrians to watch the drawbridge go up for sailboats coming from all over the world, it's not as thrilling for the cars trapped on either side. Nor is it fun for boaters who must wait for its hourly scheduled lift. Kayakers, however, always look happy—they are close enough to the water to paddle under the bridge, no matter what the state of the tide.

"Under the Drawbridge" People

National Geographic features kayakers on their Mystic webpage, yet I couldn't picture having an epic adventure in a kayak. However, being seen paddling a kayak might help me cross over from ice-cream licking tourist to a Mystic local—and one of those envied "under-the-drawbridge" people.

As I watched kayakers paddle effortlessly under the drawbridge from my usual bench in Mystic River Park (where Bailey and I sat so I could finish my daily dose of ice cream), I wondered what it would be like to be one of them. What secrets lay under the bridge?

I had tried kayaking once in upstate New York and liked it—it wasn't nearly as hard to maneuver as my rubber raft. But Jim didn't feel like renting one with me to try it out. "It looks like too much work," he said.

My break into the world of kayaking finally came when my next door neighbor Pat, feeling sorry for me being so new and friendless, invited me to the Mystic Women Club's "Dinner Club" at a local restaurant. Sitting around the table of Mystic women was newcomer Cindy. Unlike one lady who told me I would never be invited to join the Mystic Garden Club (I was caught showcasing fake red begonias in front of my house the previous winter in New York), Cindy assured me I was welcome to join her little kayaking club. She had three kayaks, a truck to transport them, and time on her hands. Like me, she was no longer raising young children.

Cindy said, "To capture the vision of being a repeat paddler, I give a frequency punch card that lists all the potential places one can go such as Mystic River, Quaimbaug Cove, Long Pond, Stonington Harbor and the Long Island Sound."[xiii]

Although I still dreamed of finding a friend with a "real" boat, the kind that would offer me a real voyage (or at least the kind of boat where no work was involved), I took Cindy up on her offer.

The biggest advantage of kayaking was that I could kayak directly to the Mystic Drawbridge Ice-Cream shop for my afternoon snack. I couldn't dock there and go inside (the dock was for the tenants above the shop), but if I ordered ahead by phone and paid by credit card, I could call from my cell phone when I arrived and an employee would run the order down to me on the river.

Another advantage of kayaking is that one doesn't need to think about what supplies to bring—there simply isn't room for anything. Even my pink visor flew off my head as we battled against the winds and outgoing tide in the Mystic River. No wonder people around here need to get parts of their face cut off every time they visit the skin doctor.

To protect myself from the sun, I bought a new kind of hat—a wide-brim khaki one with a string to hold it on under my chin. When Jim accused me of looking like I was off to shoot rhinos, it occurred to me that I should wear it everywhere. Since the media would no longer put me in the "hot babe" category, perhaps "eccentric lady" would attract their attention?

Not one to give up on my quest for a bigger boat experience, however, every time we paddled past folks relaxing on their yachts or working on their sailboats, I waved in friendship, hoping to be invited onboard. No luck—none of those boat people were interested in having me as their new buddy. They did, however, return my gaze with admiration.

Kayakers are considered cool in Mystic. As "under the drawbridge" people, kayakers depend upon no bridge tender or tide. Unlike sailors on tall, showy vessels, I held the secret to life under the drawbridge, which was a dark and cool place—and very loud with cars rumbling overhead, which were visible through the grated road. I also knew the secrets beneath the railroad swing bridge. Kayakers can go anywhere—even up close to shipwrecks since there is little danger of getting caught in the rigging. I particularly looked forward to paddling up to the partially sunken schooner, *Marmion*, now at the bottom of nearby Stonington Harbor, with only its masts and top deck partially exposed.

Kayaking was enabling me to earn my sea legs—and respect.[xiv]

On days Cindy and I weren't up to battling tides and swells, we paddled in shallow coves—especially when we brought along non-swimmers like my New York friend, Ann. A nature photographer, she brought her camera to shoot the wildlife. In addition to swans and seagulls, she said we were looking at "osprey, cormorant and the great white egret—that's the tall, skinny bird."

Despite the thrill of bird watching, I knew kayaking was not my ticket to fame and a housekeeper—there was no way I was going to attempt an Atlantic crossing in it.

Poor Cindy. I hoped she wasn't hurt knowing I was still looking for a friend with a sailboat. But really, it was for Cindy's own good I was looking for another friend, another boat. If I had a housekeeper, she wouldn't feel compelled to sweep up all the dog hair every time she came over. I had already learned the hard way that using a leaf blower indoors wasn't the way to get rid of it—especially right before guests come over and the food has already been laid out.[xv]

Cindy Modzelewski of Mystic and Elizabeth Saede of Stonington, Connecticut, prepare to paddle under the drawbridge. Avid kayakers, they are true "Under the Drawbridge" people.

7   WONDER #5: ELM GROVE CEMETERY ARCH

The "Pearly Gates?" Not exactly—these gates are made of iron, but the colossal arch to the Elm Grove Cemetery does beckon you in. Although some may be afraid to cross through the Memorial Arch to the "other" side, brides are actually sent there.

Located along the Mystic River, one hotel representative said of the cemetery, "It is the most valuable real estate in Mystic—too bad the people there can't enjoy it! But we do recommend it for wedding photography because it is so very beautiful."

This "garden cemetery" was designed in the shape of an elm tree, which is easily discernible in satellite images. Intended to be enjoyed as a park, you are invited to stroll leisurely along the river to view statues of women in flowing robes, angels, marble benches, mausoleums, plus an elegant duck pond—with some very strange looking ducks. I was almost alarmed the first time I was greeted by one with a red, lined face topped with a puffy headdress. According to James Davis, superintendent of the cemetery, the pond is home to White Pekings, Muschovies, Kyugas, Blue Swiss, and Mallards.

More than 13,000 souls, many on Mystic's "Who's Who" list of 19th century ship builders and sea captains, have been laid to rest at Elm Grove Cemetery. I became particularly interested in the tall obelisk depicting the steamship, *City of Waco*, which tells how Captain Thomas E. Wolfe died piloting her when it caught fire off the port of Galveston in 1875. The ship exploded into flames and sank—a dramatic end to a man who led an adventurous life.

During the Civil War, Wolfe had commanded the *Texana*, which transported supplies from New York to New Orleans. He was captured by the Confederates near the mouth of the Mississippi River (the Confederates showed the U.S. flag and trapped the *Texana* before Wolfe realized what was going on). The *Texana* was burned and Wolfe and his crew were taken prisoners. More than a year later, despite his weakened condition from imprisonment, he made a daring escape with some companions. Because Wolfe knew celestial navigation, he was able to find his way through enemy territory and make it back to Mystic. He was in very bad health when he arrived, and it was said that he never got over the loss of his ship. After the war, he lost another vessel, the steamship *Loyalist*, while on the way to New Orleans for repairs—but all hands were saved. When the *City of Waco* exploded and sank, everyone perished. Wolfe's body was recovered, and again he arrived back to Mystic—but this time, in a coffin.

The Elm Grove Cemetery was formally dedicated in 1854, and Mystic residents were so proud of it, that they dug up many of their dead relatives and replanted them there. In the 1890s, however, Mystic residents were outraged when the widow of a prominent shipbuilder, Charles Henry Mallory, donated funds in her husband's memory for the erection of the Memorial Arch entryway. Its construction meant the removal of two elm trees to accommodate the arch's massive span. Despite the public outcry against a manmade object replacing "nature's grand handiwork," the trees came down, stone cutters were imported from Italy, and the Memorial Arch was completed with the verse, "He Gives His Beloved Sleep," engraved across the back. Perhaps the citizens learned to appreciate the Memorial Arch after the Hurricane of 1938—for it survived, but half of the cemetery's trees did not.

Captain Sisson's Gold

Like the widow of the wealthy shipbuilder, I too faced criticism over the Elm Grove Memorial Arch. Many locals disagreed with my choice of it as a "wonder," thinking memorial arches can be seen in many other parts of the county. But there was something special about this arch—the way it stands large and alone among the trees.

It truly does summon one to enter through—or did it just summon me? As time wore on and I learned more about Mystic's dead folks, I was beginning to wonder.

Why had I been drawn to Captain Wolfe's grave in particular? Did he have something to tell me about his death on the steamship? Beside him at the cemetery lay his widow, Frances J. Sawyer, who outlived him by more than 40 years. I pondered how lonely she must have been all those years (little did I know then!).

Or, perhaps I was drawn to Elm Grove Cemetery because I felt affection for Matilda, a little two-year-old girl who drowned on New Year's

Day in 1858. There was no mystery why I found comfort visiting her grave—it reminded me of visiting our daughter Elizabeth's grave, which we had to leave behind in New York. Elizabeth died in 2006 at the age of 16 during a seizure.

Although Elizabeth was unable to walk or talk because I contracted cytomegalovirus (CMV)[xvi] when pregnant with her, she was the happiest little soul Jim and I had ever known. Missing her sweet, smiling face more than words can express, we tried to remind ourselves that she was on a better shore—one free from suffering. We had the following Scriptures etched on the back of her heart-shaped, pink headstone: "I will dwell in the house of the Lord forever," and, "then will the lame leap like a deer and the mute tongue shout for joy."

Since moving to Mystic, I was unable to visit Elizabeth's grave as often as I would have liked. On the front of Elizabeth's stone were the words, "Our Little Girl," for though she was 16, she really was very little, weighing only 50 pounds at the time of her death. Visiting the grave of little two-year-old Matilda reminded me of visiting Elizabeth—at least somewhat. But Matilda wasn't family, not mine anyway.

With the public outcry against my choice of Elm Grove Cemetery Arch as a wonder, and the suggestion that I should have chosen one of the Greek Revival or Italianate homes owned by Mystic's prosperous sea captains, I decided to learn more about those 19th century houses. Reading the little walking tour booklet, *Curbstones, Clapboards and Cupolas* [xvii], I was given a brief look at the former owners of those homes.

I was particularly interested in reading about my long-dead neighbors on West Mystic Avenue because my street, Allyn Street, was an extension of it. Suddenly, at 12 West Mystic Avenue, I came upon a last name I recognized well—Sisson. The walking tour booklet stated: *"Captain Charles Sisson bought the house in 1858 after an unsuccessful search for gold in California."*

Could it be? Was that man Sisson, who once lived down the street from me in that Italian-villa style house with a widow's walk, related to me?

I contacted my cousin, David Sisson of Rochester, New York, who had done extensive research on our Sisson line. Yes, Captain Charles Sisson was my cousin. I had family in Mystic! They might be dead, but they were mine. Captain Charles Sisson and I were fourth cousins, five times removed (both descending from Thomas and Jane Sisson). He and his wife Ann had five daughters together. [xviii]

Not only were Captain Charles Sisson and I cousins, which was enough to thrill me, but further research revealed that after his wife Ann died at sea in 1876, he married her sister— the widow of Captain Thomas E. Wolfe, the steamship pilot at Elm Grove Cemetery! Wolfe's widow, though lying next to him, hadn't lived out her years in loneliness as I had supposed—she married my cousin, who had grown up with her first husband.[xix] In fact, my cousin and Wolfe made the journey to California together in search of gold.

Sisson and Wolfe caught gold fever with another boyhood friend, Ransford Ashbey Jr., and went to California in 1850. Failing to find gold, it took Wolfe, Sisson and Ashbey nine grueling months to make it back to Mystic—but Ashbey arrived home in a coffin. Embarking from California together by steamer, they were taken to Nicaraguan Isthmus (the Panama Canal area before the canal had been built). Unable to find passage together, they split up. Sisson and Wolfe chose to trek 90 miles to the other side of the coast, where they booked passage to Key West, Florida, then onto Baltimore, Maryland. Ashbey, on the other hand, went to Chagres, where he died of tropical fever. Sisson and Wolfe arrived back in Mystic the day Ashbey's body was buried.

Later, Wolfe and Sisson married sisters Ann and Frances Sawyer. It amazed me that Sisson was such a successful sea captain by 1858 that he was able to buy that big, elegant house down the street from me. Had his search for gold truly been "unsuccessful" as the history books report?

In any case, I couldn't wait to visit the graves of Captain Charles Sisson and his first wife Ann at the Lower Mystic Cemetery along U.S. Route 1, only a mile from my house. I wouldn't be just visiting interesting dead people, I would be visiting family.

Charles and Ann Sisson's markers were not difficult to find in the small cemetery. Charles's tall stone, engraved with a sailing ship, declares, "The voyage is ended." Ann's marker is similar, and states that she died at sea on the ship *Jeremiah Thompson* at the age of 45 on May 12, 1876. Longitude and latitude were given[xx], along with the comment, "Her smile once filled our home with gladness."

When I saw a small grave marker nearby, I suddenly felt I was being shown the reason my research led me to this spot. On a stone next to Charles and Ann Sisson's was the name of their 10-month-old daughter. Engraved with "Our Little Ida," I felt I was finally given a place to grieve for our own daughter, whose marker we engraved so similarly with, "Our Little Girl."

I couldn't wait to take Jim there the following weekend—he just had to see Ida's grave marker that expressed such tender feelings. This time, the wrought iron gate to the cemetery was locked, so we had to climb over a stone wall mounted with rings for tying up horses and lined with pricker bushes. While standing in front of the Sisson markers, we saw another couple climb over the stone wall.

After the couple walked around for a while looking at headstones, the man yelled over to us, "Excuse me, would you happen to know if there are any Sissons buried here?"

Stunned, I yelled back, "Yes there are—and we're standing in front of them! I'm related to them."

The man replied, "My name is Matthew Sisson."

Unbelievably, he was my cousin too—and a living, breathing one at that! A captain in the Coast Guard stationed in nearby New London, Captain Matthew Sisson just happened to stop at this little cemetery on the off-chance he would find Sissons buried there. (Captain Matthew Sisson and I descend from Richard and Mary Sisson, an immigrant couple who were in Rhode Island by 1650).

My new-found cousin invited me to his Change of Command Ceremony in New London on June 23, 2011. Although Jim was unable to attend because it was during the workweek, I brought my kayaking friend Cindy. When we arrived, chairs had been saved up front for the Sisson family, with two reserved for us as indicated by the Sisson name taped on the back. Matthew's speech was not only thrilling because it was full of dramatic sea rescue stories, but because I was hearing it beside my new-found family of living cousins.

Months after I posted my Sisson encounter on my blog, I was stunned to receive an e-mail from a man who had been searching online for information on the ship, *Jeremiah Thompson* (the one Ann Sisson had died on in 1876). Apparently, he had the original ship model of the *Jeremiah Thompson*, which he inherited from his father.

The gentleman and I excitedly e-mailed back and forth about the model, and I went back to Ann's stone to make sure I had given him the correct coordinates where Ann died en route from San Francisco, California, to Liverpool, England. Confused on some points about longitude and latitude, I e-mailed my Coast Guard cousin Captain Matthew Sisson with some questions. When I remarked about the frequency of deaths at sea on several of the other grave markers in the cemetery, he replied, "Mystic was a hard place, and the headstones and memorials tell a hard story."

As a result of an earlier edition of this book, another person connected to Captain Charles and Ann Sawyer Sisson contacted me—Judey Sawyer Buckbee, a relative of Ann and Frances Sawyer. She too had been drawn to their headstones. To my delight, she shared some of her hard-won information with me. She said, "I am sure that both Ann and Charles are still trying to tell their story and our meeting is just another great piece of it."

Was my long-dead cousin, Captain Charles C. Sisson, working from beyond the grave to tell me something because I was his only living relative in Mystic?

Unbeknownst to me, a distant cousin of mine, genealogist Carol Sisson Regehr, had looked for Captain Sisson's descendants in order to give them the family Bible (she received from Col. John Sisson who got it from a Connecticut antique dealer). After a brief search through genealogical records, Carol was unable to locate any living descendants, so John and Carol donated it to the Collections Research Center at Mystic Seaport where Sisson's papers and ship journals are kept.

Carol said, "I'm glad there was a home for the Bible at the museum. Otherwise, I don't know how far afield I would have had to go to find a sideways relative who might have wanted it."

Although I may only be Captain Charles Sisson's "sideways" relative, perhaps he was trying to tell me that he and his friend Captain Wolfe actually found gold in California and buried it somewhere nearby. Maybe even on my property? If it wasn't Captain Sisson trying to reach me from beyond the grave, maybe it was his and Wolfe's third companion on their gold-seeking venture, Ransford Ashby. Did Ashby want me to know what really happened to him on his way back to Mystic from California? He was buried near Captain Sisson, so I had gotten into the habit of visiting—and wondering—about him too.

Or, did Captain Charles Sisson's first wife, Ann, want me to know the cause of her death at sea on the *Jeremiah Thompson*? Had she met a foul end so her husband would be free to pursue her widowed sister?

I searched for clues in Captain Sisson's journal of the voyage held at the Mystic Seaport Collections Resource Center. Although his writing was difficult to read, I could make out a few words—ones that indicated Ann suffered at the end and left behind a husband deep in grief. The day of her death he writes, *"During the afternoon my Dear Wife gradually grows weaker...I could see a great change in her face."* Sisson records that at the end, Ann said, *"God help You and the Dear Children..."*[xxi] The following day, Saturday, May 13, 1876, after commenting on the weather at sea, Sisson writes that Ann is *"gone never to return and is I trust in Heaven free from pain and sorrow. Never can I forget the closing scene..."*[xxii] On May 26: *"How I long to see the end of this unfortunate voyage."*[xxiii] On June 4: *"It is one month today since my Dear Wife had her first* [two illegible words] *which she only survived for 8 days... she is now at rest and I am left to toil on for a while longer."*[xxiv] According to the *Norwich Courier* dated July 5, 1876, Ann's preserved body arrived home by steamer from Liverpool. Charles followed on a later steamer.

In my quest to learn more about Captain Charles Sisson, I found several books that highlighted his career. I discovered that Sisson was master and part owner of the clipper ship, *Elizabeth F. Willets*, which was launched in Mystic in 1854. Well known for her fast delivery times between ports, the *Elizabeth F. Willets* is portrayed in its early stages of construction at Mystic Seaport's large, 50-foot diorama of the Mystic River community during the mid-1800s.

I visited the exhibit often, wondering if it revealed clues to any Sisson gold or family secrets. As I studied the landscape of 250 detailed buildings, complete with little people, horse-drawn wagons, outhouses, and the oxen that moved the drawbridge, I felt like the dreamer in an old *Twilight Zone* episode who got sucked back in time into a doll house exhibit. If I ever "go missing," you'll know where to look.

According to the book, *Greyhounds of the Sea*, Sisson didn't make the best time between New York and San Francisco on the *Elizabeth F. Willets*. Sisson himself said he was the "Black Sheep" compared to the other ships that left approximately the same time he did on Jan. 13, 1855. He wrote: *"May 10—3 P.M. Anchored S.F. 118 days and 3 hours from New York, and found that I was the Black Sheep out of the fleet. The* Neptune's Car *102 days, the* Westward Ho *102 days and the bark [a type of ship]* Greenfield *110 days."* Apparently, Sisson hit a calm belt off the coast of California and it took him 15 days to cover the remaining 800 miles of the trip.

The author of *Greyhounds of the Sea*, however, offered another explanation of Sisson's slow time: *"It is possible that Sisson was too preoccupied with a disciplinary problem to make a fast passage. Just before leaving home to join his ship on this voyage he had warned his small daughter that if she left the yard without permission he would punish her. Shortly before his departure the little girl was missing and he was compelled to leave before he had a chance to make good his word. On his return a year later his first act was to lay the culprit over his knee and administer a sound spanking."*[xxv]

This little anecdote presented another mystery. According to the family Bible, Captain Sisson didn't have children at the time of that particular voyage. Perhaps the author of the book simply got the spanking year wrong? If this daughter did exist, she would have been Charles and Ann's firstborn—but I highly doubt they would have forgotten to record their firstborn in the Bible. Could she be a child of Charles's from another union? Is she trying to let me know that Sisson does have a living direct descendent somewhere?

Captain Sisson's life seemed surrounded by mystery—and death. I can't imagine being the parents of the 15-year-old boy who went from New York to San Francisco with him. Sisson's name was etched on their son's grave marker placed in his memory: "John Lamphere, born May 2, 1842, Lost in the Pacific Ocean from Ship Mary E. Sutton, Capt. Sisson, June 20, 1857" (Wichtman burying ground, Cold Springs Rd., Old Mystic, CT).

Despite the death of the young boy in his charge, Sisson must have been highly regarded by those who knew him best. Prior to the death of his gold-seeking companion Captain Thomas Wolfe, Thomas and Frances had entrusted Sisson with their 14-year-old son, Charles Herbert Wolfe, who served as ship's boy when Sisson commanded *Bridgewater*. It was on the *Bridgewater* in April of 1871 that Sisson came upon the sinking Swedish bark, *Belladonna,* and rescued the captain, two mates and 48 seamen.

In order to better understand any clues that the Mystic Seaport diorama might hold on the lives and wives of Captain Charles Sisson and his friends, I needed to know Mystic's ship building and seafaring history. With ships given people names, I came to view the famous ships of Mystic's yesteryear as adventurers and explorers themselves.

After the American Revolution, ship building grew as a major industry along Mystic River because the river is deep enough, its banks slope gently to the water, and the area is protected from the worst of Atlantic Ocean storms by Fishers Island. According to a plaque in Mystic Seaport's Mystic River Scale Model exhibit, which represents one mile along the River from the 1850s through the 1870s, Mystic "produced a greater tonnage of ships and steamers than any place its size in America."

One of Mystic's early history-making ships was the sloop *Hero* built in 1800 as a coastal trader. Used during the War of 1812, she served as a privateer and blockade runner and once helped recapture another Mystic-built vessel. One of her captains during the war, Jeremiah Holmes, had previously been captured when out at sea and pressed into service (basically kidnapped) by the British Royal Navy.[xxvi] Escaping after three years, Holmes later joined other local militia volunteers in defeating the British at the Battle of Stonington. The *Hero* was eventually captured herself by the British. After the war, the 47.5 foot *Hero* was re-outfitted as a sealer (a ship used for hunting seals).

On November 17, 1820, when the *Hero* pressed further south in search of new seal breeding grounds, her then commander, Captain Nathaniel B. Palmer, sighted "*land not yet laid down on my chart.*"[xxvii] Palmer and his crew of four had discovered Antarctica. Now a museum, the Nathanial B. Palmer House of Stonington certainly deserved a spot on my Mystic Seafarer's Trail. (Remember, my Seafarer's Trail isn't just Mystic and its wonders. It encompasses the haunts and homes of noted seafarers in nearby Stonington and Noank as well.)

When the California Gold Rush became headline news, attracting the likes of my cousin Charles Sisson and friends, Mystic shipbuilders worked to meet the demand for clipper ships. Clippers, with their hulls designed to slice through water and abundance of sails, "clipped" more than a month off the time it took to get from the northeast to California. The 13,000-mile trip from New York to San Francisco, by way of Cape Horn off South

America, normally took more than four months. On a clipper, the trip could be made in as little as three months. (Those Gold Fever folks didn't have the Panama Canal to speed their trip—it wasn't completed until 1914.)

Mystic became noted for their "half clippers" or "medium clippers," which incorporated a hull design by an orphan from Stonington (Mason C. Hill) that allowed for greater storage space while still meeting the need for speed. One of the most celebrated and profitable Mystic-built clippers was the *David Crockett,* named after America's famous pioneer. Built in 1853, it was immortalized in a sailor song describing life on board as a "floating Hell." Called the "Leaving of Liverpool," the song portrays a sailor's dread of leaving his lady and the notoriously tough working conditions under Captain John Burgess.[xxviii] Captain Burgess' reign of terror finally ended on his 1874 trip from San Francisco to Liverpool, England, to deliver a cargo of wheat. His departure was delayed five days because of a mutiny, and once at sea, he was washed overboard (or pushed?) and drowned in a gale off South America.

Rounding South America, particularly the island of Cape Horn, wasn't just dangerous for the likes of Captain Burgess; it was the dread of every sailor—and still is. The waterway between South America and the ice off Antarctica is one of the most hazardous in the world to navigate. Known as the "sailors' graveyard," the waters are fraught with strong winds and currents, large waves, and icebergs.

The *David Crockett* herself never succumbed to Cape Horn and was consistently fast, making the trip between San Francisco and New York in as little as 93 days in 1860 (the captain of her on that trip, Peter E. Rowland, lived next door to Captain Sisson at #10 West Mystic Ave.). The *David Crockett* made a lot of money in its 46-year career, netting more than a half-million dollars in the first half of it. She met her end when she ran aground on a shoal in New York Bay in 1899. It took a week of winter gales to break her apart. The shipyard where the *David Crockett* was built is now the site of Mystic Seaport, and the spot where her keel was laid is marked by a large rock and plaque. Mystic Seaport's historic diorama features her near-completed construction on land and highlights how enormous she was compared to the other ships being built at that time—including my cousin's ship, the *Elizabeth F. Willets,* shown in its early stages. (Is that why Sisson made a slow passage to California in the *Elizabeth F. Willets*—he suffered from "ship envy?")

Although we know how the *David Crockett* met her end, there are other Mystic-built ships that simply disappeared. Mystic cemeteries are full of markers engraved with anchors and "Lost at Sea." While visiting the dead Sissons, I noticed a large stone placed as a memorial to Captain Charles H. Gates and his 18-year-old son. It stated that father and son were last seen on the *Cremorne* leaving San Francisco on June 1, 1870, bound for

Liverpool, England, and they "were never heard from." In addition to them, 22 other crew members were lost at sea.

Did they join all the others who found their eternal rest in the sailor's graveyard off Cape Horn? The *Cremorne* had been advertised as superior in strength to the *David Crockett*. If that's true, perhaps the *Cremorne* will be found someday, a ghost ship still sailing the high seas. (This has happened before. In 1872, the brigantine *Mary Celeste* was found abandoned yet still sailing the Atlantic. Food and personal belongings were intact, but passengers and crew had simply disappeared.)

Before Captain Charles H. Gates went missing, he had lived near me at 48 New London Road (U.S. Route 1). His wife, Jane E. (Latham) Gates, sold their home 12 years after his disappearance. Never remarrying, she was finally reunited with her husband and son upon her death 53 long years later. She is buried near the stone honoring their memory in Lower Mystic Cemetery.

Although Cape Horn is the final resting place for many captains, there was a Mystic captain who lived on 77 High Street who defied the odds. According to Bill Peterson, Mystic historian, "Joseph Warren Holmes [son of Jeremiah Holmes of the *Hero*] has the distinction of rounding Cape Horn safely 84 times as a sailing ship master. This is a record that still stands." From 1857-1859, Joseph W. Holmes was the captain of the *Elizabeth F. Willets*, the one part owned by my cousin, Captain Sisson. I was amazed how intertwined Sisson's life was with all the folks I had been stumbling across in my research.

Now, like Captain Charles Sisson, Captain Joseph W. Holmes is peacefully moldering in his grave. Unlike the other seafarers who had captured my imagination, they were not "lost at sea" with only their shoes left lying on the ocean floor as markers.

Mystic's shipbuilding industry grew to an all-time high during the Civil War with the construction of 57 steamships—the largest output in New England apart from Boston. Purchased or chartered by the government, the ships were used as gunboats and troop transports. After the Southern states rejoined the Union, Mystic shipbuilding eventually gave way to the production of wool, velvet, and tar soap. Those industries have since given way to tourism, award-winning restaurants, trendy shops and museums (but if you want to learn more about those things, you will have to read someone else's book!).

Now onto more Mystic wonders and adventurers—some who are still very much alive.

8   WONDER #6: MYSTIC PIZZA RESTAURANT SIGN

Although this "wonder" may not have been considered by the ancient Greek historians, how could I not choose the lighted restaurant sign, "Mystic Pizza: A Slice of Heaven," when the majority of tourists ask me, "Where is Mystic Pizza?"

Although it's been more than 20 years since the release of the 1988 romantic comedy, *Mystic Pizza*, starring Julia Roberts and debuting Matt Damon (whose only line, "Mom, do you want my green stuff?" was said while eating lobster), visitors still flock to the restaurant that inspired it.

When Jim and I had dinner there for the first time, we sat in the front window to watch the pedestrians stroll past. I actually got to feel what it must be like to be famous—everyone outside was taking our picture! At first, I wondered if the tourists thought I was Julia Roberts. It wasn't until I got out of my chair and got a closer look that I realized they weren't taking pictures of me; it was the Mystic Pizza sign!

The Zelepos family, owners of Mystic Pizza, state, "Incredibly, our little pizza shop caught the eye of screenwriter Amy Jones, who was summering in the area. Ms. Jones chose Mystic Pizza as the focus and setting for her story of the lives and loves of three young waitresses." The movie depicts life in a small fishing village and was filmed in Mystic and the surrounding communities.

The locals will never forget the day that Hollywood came to town—just ask Mystic shopkeepers and waiters what it was like to accommodate the 80-member film crew. Most have a story to tell—how the bridge operator needed to raise the drawbridge on cue; how local fishermen advised actors on stringing bait; or how they have a friend whose family moved into a hotel while a scene was shot in their home. Local racing sailor Katie Bradford said, "I'm friends with Skip, the guy who was actually steering the boat in the Mystic River scene. He had to do it lying on his back so an actor would appear as though he was steering." Katie also tells how another friend became a local celebrity—simply because the back of his head made it into the movie!

For those who have never seen the film, they can have their chance by peering into the restaurant where it plays continuously on three screens. "It's on mute—otherwise, we'd go nuts!" confided one waitress.

The restaurant sells souvenirs (as well as pizza) and proudly displays movie photos, posters and newspaper clippings featuring the restaurant. The waitresses even have a little fun by dressing up a mannequin as Daisy, the Julia Roberts character in the film. They change her hair accessories to match the colors of the season.

More than 20 years after the movie's release, film production companies still can't get enough of Mystic Pizza. Restaurant co-owner John Zelepos recently received a call from California asking if his restaurant and family would star in a reality TV show.

How To Get in a Movie (or how not to)

Since Hollywood, as well as several other film makers, still come to Mystic to make movies when they need a quaint seaport village or historic, tall ships in the background, it made me think. Maybe I was destined to become a famous movie star—not a famous adventurer!

Yet how could I get in a movie when I was rarely selected for even the smallest of speaking parts in high school productions? Many years after high school, it finally occurred to me that if I wanted to get a part, I would have to write and produce my own play. So, I published excerpts of my ancestor's Civil War love letters into a "reader's theater." I starred myself as my 17-year-old great-great grandmother—despite being over 40 at the time.

It didn't work—Hollywood remained strangely quiet after my debut.

But here, living in a popular film setting, maybe a casting agent would see Bailey and me walking down the street and shout, "Stop that lady and her hound!"

Hearing the next major movie to be shot in Mystic was "Hope Springs," starring Meryl Streep, Tommy Lee Jones and Steve Carell, I began plotting to get in it—even if it was just the back of my head!

Just as I was pondering how I could get a small role in the film, I received an e-mail from Kristin of Mystv Studios. Mystv Studios is a local production company that makes commercials and the travel show, "Mystic Coast Connection," which plays continuously in 4,000 area hotels. I had met Kristin at a networking event hosted by the Greater Mystic Chamber of Commerce, a gathering where I had hoped to meet potential clients in need of a writer—or a friend with a boat. Kristin had no boat, but she had another vehicle to launch me from obscurity.

Kristin's e-mail to me:

"I was wondering if you'd be interested in helping out on a commercial shoot at a local casino. You and I would be P.A.'s, so we'll be fetching and holding light screens, checking off the shot list, and various other unglamorous things. It might be fun and I *know* it would be more fun for me if you were there!"

I had no idea what a P.A. was, and was only being asked because I might be "fun," but I certainly wasn't going to reject a chance to squeeze my image somewhere onto this film!

Scheming how to go from P.A. to film star (or at least film "extra"), I watched reruns of "I Love Lucy" to study Lucy's sneaky antics that landed her roles in Ricky's shows. Sometimes she didn't have to bind and gag a competing actress and stuff her into a closet—sometimes it just took fitting into the right costume. Maybe if I wore the right outfit, I could catch the director's eye. Having little fashion sense, I asked Jim, who usually arranges my outfits when I need to look presentable, what I should wear.

Just as I was pondering this, I received another e-mail from Kristin: "You might be asked to be 'peanuts,' meaning filler for the commercial, so make sure your husband dresses you." There was hope I'd get in this commercial—and without any devious plotting!

On the morning of the shoot, I learned a whole new industry (such as P.A. means Production Assistant)—and that almost anyone can get into a film as an extra (or a "peanut"). If a person has talent, they can get paying roles as a "principal" or a "secondary" in practical films such as training videos. One actress at the shoot was using her downtime in the green room (a spot designated for actors to relax between takes) to practice a five-page monologue for her upcoming role as an organ transplant recipient in an educational film. I felt sorry for the organ recipient she was playing—if I went through the terror of receiving someone else's body part, I would want to star in my own film about it!

I was told just before the shoot that a "grip" had been hired, so I wouldn't be needed to hold and carry film equipment. Still wanting to look official, I brought my own clipboard—and it worked! Appearing like a person in authority, the actors came to me with important questions that ranged from "Where is the bathroom?" to "Do you think my scene will be shot soon?" One woman, an extra, wanted to leave for a while to hang out in the smoking area. I reminded her that the slot machine scene, which required extras, was scheduled soon.

She replied, "Someone else told me it wouldn't be for an hour or so."

Sure enough, right after she left, I got word it was time for the extras to leave for their scene. I told the director I would take her place (it's a dog eat dog world out there), but was told to stay where I was.

Kristin told me not to despair—they might still need me to heap food on my plate in the buffet scene or to dance in the nightclub scene. Since I didn't want to admit I was a terrible, uncoordinated dancer, I stressed that I would be just perfect for the buffet scene. Not to brag, but I did win first place in a New Jersey pie eating contest—twice! (Okay, it was 40 years ago when I was a kid, but I'm still very good at eating pie.)

As I feared, I was not given the chance to shine in the buffet scene, but was needed on the dance floor of the nightclub scene. I felt awkward and uncoordinated as I pranced around to the music alongside the hot babes featured in the commercial. I guess the director couldn't bear to watch me anymore and politely said, "Now you dance in the back—look as though you are still trying to 'find your way.'"

I guess that's true—I am still trying to "find my way!"

The commercial was aired during the TV show, *Wheel of Fortune*, but I knew it wouldn't make me a star. It took several viewings before I caught a split-second glimpse of my yellow and blue skirt flashing by in the background. I doubted a director for the upcoming Meryl Streep movie would see that and get inspired to track me down. Back to the drawing board.

Advised to register with talent agencies such as New England Actors, I was alarmed to read I would have to reveal my weight to sign up. No movie was worth that! I was simply going to have to lose a lot of weight before registering for that talent agency—or any other.

9   WONDER #7: MYSTIC TRAIN DEPOT

Whether you arrive by Amtrak's Northeast Regional train, or are biking past the Mystic Train Depot, you may wonder, "Haven't I seen this before?"

Yes, you may have—and you may have even played with a miniature version of it. Constructed in 1905, the Mystic Train Depot served as the inspiration for American Flyer's "talking" toy train stations made in the mid-1900s. Now a collector's item, the toy model bearing the name "Mystic" can be viewed and even touched at the Mystic Train Depot. When I pressed the button on the model, I heard a far-a-way, long-ago train whistle and a conductor announce in a crackly voice, "All aboard...New York, Philadelphia, Chicago and all points west. Aboard!"

Over its long history, the Depot has seen many reunions—some not so happy. According to the book, *Mystic in the 1950s* by Tom Santos, "During the Korean War, in the early fifties, bodies were shipped home by train. Mr. Sam Pettini was the shipping agent, he received the casket containing the body of a soldier, the VFW sent members to meet the train and take the body to wherever it had to go."

Now, the Mystic Train Depot is not only where people come and go by locomotive, it's the very epicenter of every Mystic area adventure *National Geographic* says is possible. When you step inside the Depot, you step inside the Welcome Center sponsored by the Greater Mystic Chamber of Commerce.

Here, you will find every imaginable "Mystic Country" map and brochure possible—you will find information about fishing charters, pleasure cruises, tall ships, submarines, lighthouses, hiking, kayaking, wineries, museums, where to sleep, shop, gamble, eat, drink beer, cider or lick ice cream. Free bike "rentals" are available (through Mystic Community Bikes) as well as discount tickets to Mystic Seaport and to the Mystic Aquarium.

I visited this spot often when we moved to Mystic because I love brochures. Not just the smell of them, but how they take me places I've never been, but hope to. I also enjoyed talking to the tourist advisors stationed behind the desk—they are full of behind-the-scenes secrets. One young man Dave volunteered at the Center simply because he loves the area. Well-read, he delights in sharing his little-known secrets with others. He said, "I love seeing the look on visitors' faces when they discover something neat about Mystic."

Upon hearing I wanted more information on the Great Hurricane of 1938 because it had altered so many of the Mystic sites I had been researching, Dave told me to read the book, *Sudden Sea*, by R.A. Scotti—especially if I wanted to learn about the tragic train derailment of the *Bostonian* on a causeway between Mystic and Stonington.

Apparently, it was because of the bravery of the brakeman that more people weren't washed away when the storm surge trapped them on the causeway. Also brave was a group of prep school boys and an MIT student who helped passengers move to the safer, forward cars. Thanks to the brakeman, who plunged under five feet of water to uncouple the front cars from the flooded, derailed cars, only two perished.

Of the two who died on the *Bostonian*, one was an older woman who panicked when the train became trapped on the causeway. She jumped into the storm surge and never came up, possibly trapped by the loose homes and boats slamming against the train (of the 52 vessels in the Stonington commercial fishing fleet, 50 were completely destroyed).

The body of the pantryman was later found in the garden of a private home in Stonington.

What the *Bostonian* passengers saw happening around them would never be forgotten. A Brown University senior reported that he watched helplessly as a woman and her two children clung to each other in the remains of their home that went floating nearby.

Suddenly, the walls and floor fell apart, and the little family went down into the roiling sea.

Hurricane Irene of 2011

Now that I lived closer to the Atlantic Ocean than ever before, would I have more hurricanes to fear? Although I would never admit it to anyone in Mystic, I thought it would be kind of exciting to experience a New England hurricane (but only the kind where no one died). A good hurricane survival story just might be my ticket to a *New York Times* bestseller—and the kind of notoriety I sought in order to promote a cause dear to my heart. (Amelia Earhart used her fame to promote women's rights; my cause is a mother's right to know how to protect her unborn child from congenital CMV.) [xxix]

Several years before moving to Mystic, I had watched the dramatic story of the Moore family during the Hurricane of 1938 on television. Parents with their four children (plus two others) clung to the top floor of their home as it sailed from Rhode Island clear across Little Narragansett Bay to Barn Island, Connecticut, which is very close to Mystic. A wildlife management area with hiking trails, Bailey and other dogs like to meet there to stroll through the salt marsh together.

Although I had a good hurricane story too (Hurricane Floyd of 1999), it never got the kind of press the Moore family's got because I didn't nearly drown. Thank goodness it was less dramatic than their story because it involved our daughter Elizabeth—she and I were trapped on a train amidst the rising waters. [xxx]

Just as I was about to despair that nothing exciting was ever going to happen to me in Mystic, I got the news—Mystic would receive a direct hit from Hurricane Irene at the end of August.

Secretly thrilled, I raced to the store with everyone else to stock up on batteries and milk. Then, following instructions from newscasters, we battened down the hatches (not sure yet what that means exactly, but we tied down our lawn furniture). Taking Bailey on several walks a day to downtown Mystic, I watched shopkeepers board up their windows and position sandbags to prepare for the possibility of the Mystic River overflowing its banks. Friends who worked along the Thames River told of watching submarines from the Naval Submarine base going out to sea where they would fare better during the storm.

Excitement was at its peak when the Weather Channel came to the Mystic drawbridge on Saturday, August 27, 2011, the day before the hurricane was scheduled to hit. They were filming boats sailing up Mystic River in search of better protection from the expected storm surge.

I positioned myself in front of the Weather Channel's camera crew and tried to look like a concerned yacht or tall ship owner. All hopes of a reporter wanting to interview me about my storm preparations were dashed when the camera man moved his equipment to another spot to get me out of his line of sight.

I heard later that the Mystic River was featured on national news, but I doubted I even made it into the background. No hope for the directors of the upcoming Meryl Streep movie to spot me there.

Although secretly disappointed late Saturday when I learned the hurricane would only be a tropical storm by the time it hit Mystic, I still tossed and turned most of the night listening to the approaching storm—what if our brook flooded the house?

The worst of the storm hit Sunday morning. I pulled on my tall rubber boots at dawn and endured the pelting rain and tree limb-ripping wind to clear the storm drain on our property (Jim, a deep sleeper, had no idea I was risking my life to save our property). Although I knew Hurricane Irene wouldn't give me the bestseller I hoped for, what happened afterwards gave me plenty to blog about for days—which all had to be done from Starbucks, my new home office.

Blog post:
Monday, August 29—Day one after Hurricane Irene
No serious flooding here in Mystic as we got more wind than rain. There are many trees and limbs down, however, which knocked out our power—for a week or more we were told.

Jim and I were lucky our brook didn't flood our home or the neighborhood. I went out all morning during the storm to keep the drain free of debris, wearing knee-high rubber boots so I could step into the stream and rip away vines, branches, etc. Perhaps stupidly, I walked Bailey downtown during the storm and kept storm drains clear in the streets as well. I single-handedly saved Mystic from flooding, but since I was out alone, no one but Bailey knows!

Our oven is electric and we don't have a propane grill, but Mystic Pizza has a generator, so we had a hot meal Sunday night—along with the rest of the Mystic locals. Most of the tourists had evacuated by then.

With the power out, the traffic lights don't work, so driving around is difficult. The drawbridge can't go up either, so boats are trapped.

I'm tempted to spend the entire day at Starbucks to keep my laptop/cell phone charged—and you all informed—but in fairness to everyone else, I should only take an outlet for a maximum of two hours. I still write for Rockland Community College and have deadlines, which requires me to have Internet service, so I must use the power and Internet service I get at Starbucks for that.

Blog post:
Tuesday, August 30—Day three after Hurricane Irene

Perhaps you are hearing how Connecticut is having trouble getting power back on because of the shortage of linemen. According to an announcement from the governor, Connecticut Light and Power "was still searching for available crews as far away as Seattle or British Columbia." So if you, my dear reader, need a job, become a lineman!

I'm still writing to you from Starbucks. The people sitting around me drinking coffee look like they've been camping. Many are on well water so don't have any running water at all as it is electrically pumped. Others, like me, have running water and showers, but can't stand putting their heads under the cold water. I still have shampoo on my scalp from my first cold shower—I just couldn't stand under the water long enough to get all the soap out.

The night sky never looked better from our house. With a new moon and no lights from town, the stars are spectacular. Occasionally, we see a faint glow in a driveway, which always turns out to be a DVD player plugged into the car battery. Family members gather in their car for an evening of entertainment and to cook with hot plates. Jim and I have been curling up in bed with my Starbuck's charged laptop to watch DVDs. Last night we finished the movie, *The Mothman Prophecies*, a scary movie about impending doom. The previous evening, my laptop ran out of power just at the climax.

Yesterday, I bought a folding stove at the Army Navy Store. It sits over a canned flame and takes forever to cook anything. Because I was writing for the college until 6:45 p.m. at Starbucks, Jim had to start dinner by frying up some of our rapidly defrosting meat, in this case, turkey burgers. I took one bite and couldn't eat anymore—it tasted slimy from the frying pan (Jim thinks the flame made it taste funny, but I don't see how). Anyway, I asked him if he'd mind if I gave my turkey burger to Bailey. Upset, Jim said, "I slaved all night over this hot flame and you're giving your dinner to the dog?"

What I really wanted was yummy movie popcorn for dinner, so after giving my turkey burgers to Bailey, I talked Jim into seeing a film at the Olde Mistick Village Theater. It was comforting to sit with the other dirty heads in Mystic eating warm popcorn. I don't remember what we saw, but I do remember the popcorn.

I decided to buy a spray at a hair salon that is supposed to make your hair look like it's been washed. It's called "Dirty Secret." If you want to know whether it keeps my dirty little hair secret a secret, just keep checking back to my blog. [I wasn't sure if the status of my hair would keep people reading my blog, but I was desperate to keep my audience before some new weather disaster hit another part of the country.]

Blog post:

Thursday, September 1—Day five after Hurricane Irene, dirty hair tackled by government

Still no power, no hot water—and no one wants to shower. Still no oven, so we've been gathering nightly with our marginally showered friends by candlelight at a friend's house with a propane grill to cook our rotting meat and slurp our soggy, previously frozen vegetables and fruit.

Possibly as a result of businesses complaining to the government that tourists won't come back to Mystic if its residents won't bathe, we were ordered to take advantage of free showers. I'm not kidding, this is a Groton Patch headline: "Groton Respite Center Wants Town, Region To Take Showers." The government provided trailers with curtained off sections for showering. They even offered residents a free, hot meal as an enticement to step into these barely private stalls with shower heads that pointed to one's private parts (one teenage girl blogged about how embarrassing it was to shower with her mother and sister).

Although I learned how to take a cold shower without going into shock (I do a backbend so only my head goes under the spray), I'm dying to try one of those lack-of-privacy showers offered in the trailer just so I can see what it's like.

As I'm writing to you from Starbucks, I'm listening to some grumpy, older men who are complaining about Connecticut's lack of lineman to get the power back on. Yesterday, the radio played the old song, "The Wichita Lineman." The mayor got on the air and told us to give "thumbs up" signs to all the bucket trucks that drive by.

Well, I must get going on my college writing work before I get kicked out of Starbucks for charging my laptop and cell phone too long while sipping only one cup of coffee.

Rotting Meat Potlucks

While the power was out, for three nights in a row, Jim and I and our new, barely showered friends, checked our fridges for spoiling food to contribute to kayaker Cindy and husband Gary's nighty grilling parties. Watching Gary flip pounds of scallops, shrimp and chicken over their large, state-of-the-art propane gas grill was great for a joke. Here he was, an engineer at the local nuclear power plant, yet he couldn't get electricity to his own house. "I just make the power," Gary said, "I don't distribute it."

Since no one wanted to rush home after dinner to a dark house, we spent hours getting to know each other through the telling of our life stories. One thing became very clear as those evenings unfolded—Jim and I had lived a very dull, routine life.

Gary and Cindy regaled us with their recent kayaking adventures, including one where they were nearly swept out into the Atlantic when fighting a difficult battle against the outgoing tide in a Rhode Island salt water pond. (Note to self: the next time I go kayaking with Cindy, text Jim at work so he'll know where to start looking if I don't come home.)

Then there was Kate, who told of giving birth on a schooner she built with her husband. She rowed to shore the next day to weigh her daughter, Araminta, on a scale in the Ford's lobster shack seen in the movie, *Mystic Pizza*. Their schooner is now featured in the pen and ink drawing on the label of the locally brewed beer, Mystic Bridge IPA. The artwork was done by her artist son, Clem. As Kate described the difficult process of building their schooner from keel up in her backyard, she answered several questions about the ingenious ways she and her husband found and cobbled together the rest of the boat. After several minutes of discussing boat construction from stem to stern, Jim, tired of being too lost to join in, finally asked, "What's a keel?"

Suddenly, the whole party exploded in laughter as they realized how long Jim must have been confused—that he didn't even know the basics, that a keel is the backbone of the ship—its very foundation. I felt bad I had forgotten to warn Jim not to ask boating questions like that in public—not in Mystic anyway.

Trying to move the crowd away from humiliating Jim further, Kate changed the subject to the time she and her husband earned a living oyster fishing on their rebuilt 1904 skipjack. They named their oldest child after the most famous boat builder in the world, Noah, because he was born exactly one week after they launched their skipjack.

Kate eventually left her life on the sea to become an acupuncturist and Chinese herbalist. Whenever any of us at the dinner party complained of an ache or pain, she wanted to stick us with needles or concoct some sort of herbal brew. Jim probably could have used a needle sticking session to help him get over his lingering embarrassment over his keel question. Not one to draw attention to himself, I knew Jim wouldn't be telling any of his stories to this seafaring crowd—especially not in front of Jules and Neil.

Most recently from New Orleans, Jules and her fiancé Neil were new to the area because Neil was transferred to Naval Submarine Base New London (located in Groton). Neil, a career Navy man, had lived on the edge for years—and so had Jules. Just like Amelia Earhart, Jules was a social worker and an adventuress.

I first met Jules walking Bailey over the Mystic drawbridge. When she told me she grew up in Alaska and spent her Saturdays shooting off guns with her dad before heading out for ice-cream, I knew she'd make an interesting friend. She even ate an intruding bear shot by her father.

At the Hurricane Irene dinner party, Jules told us what it was like to live in New Orleans during Hurricane Katrina. Instead of folks happily sitting around sharing defrosted food, bodies were being tied to street signs and telephone poles. Permanent ink was used on the skin to state where it had been found.

Although she didn't have a boat, Jules had been sailing since she was a teenager. Neil didn't like to admit it to his Navy buddies, but it was Jules who taught him how to sail. As Jules told of their adventures kayaking, rock climbing, wilderness camping, and teaching Special Olympic athletes how to sail, I thought Jules was even more daring than Amelia Earhart—because she accomplished all of that completely blind (not just legally blind). Her life reminded me of that famous quote about dancer Ginger Rogers: "Sure [Fred Astaire] was great, but don't forget Ginger Rogers did everything he did backwards...and in high heels!"[xxxi]

I wondered how I would ever compete with Jules's stories when it was my turn to hold the floor. And what about poor Jim, a reserved scientist? His most exciting childhood experiences were pretending he was Captain Kirk aboard the Starship Enterprise. Neil, on the other hand, served aboard the real *USS ENTERPRISE,* the world's oldest nuclear powered air craft carrier. He was deployed in two wars, Desert Fox and Desert Shield. He held us captive with his stories of life at sea in the Middle East as Scud missiles flew overhead.

Pondering my story telling counter-attack, I wondered if I should talk about my writing work at Rockland Community College. Should I tell them about the inspiring stories I regularly uncovered of students persisting against unimaginable odds to get their education? One young woman, Jordan (Jody), told me how earning her degree meant she not only had to study 10 times harder than everyone else to compensate for learning disabilities, but having her legs amputated at the age of 13 meant she had to get around campus in a wheelchair. When trying to help a man who dropped his soda, she fell out of her wheelchair, losing her prosthetic legs in the process. Jody, determined to help others enjoy life despite their physical challenges, is now the inspiration behind and director of the Forever Jordan Foundation, an organization that raises funds for disabled children.

Not sure if this crowd would think Jody's story qualified as "my" story, I decided to bring out my standby party stopper—the story of how our daughter Jackie and hound Bailey found a dead body.[xxxii]

I finished the tale with my worry about how disturbed Jackie must have been when she realized she had been alone in the woods with a dead man—especially one who had hung himself. I had said to Jackie, "Oh, you poor thing—you must be so upset!"

Jackie's response to me? "Oh, I'm fine, I've always wanted to find a dead body!"

Once my captive audience got over the shock of Jackie's response and my confession that I, too, wanted to find a dead body, the conversation stalled.

Since Jim wasn't one for being the center of attention, I decided, as his wife, I should be allowed to take his place and tell another long story. When I glanced at the bottles of Samuel Adams Boston Lager on the table, I found my topic.

Pointing to the beer, I said, "If Sam Adams had his way, I wouldn't exist." With my audience looking confused but intrigued, I continued with how Adams wanted my ancestor, Captain Henry Gale, a Revolutionary War veteran, to hang for his leadership role in Shays' Rebellion (he tried to stop courts from prosecuting farmers who couldn't pay their high taxes and debts after the war).

After quoting excerpts from his father and wife's futile letters to the governor of Massachusetts seeking his pardon, I came to the climax: "In the end, it was decided that each county should hang at least one leader of Shays' Rebellion. It was determined that Henry Gale should hang for Worchester County. So, he was marched up the gallows, a noose placed around his neck, and prayers were said for his soul. Just as he was about to drop out of the land of the living, the sheriff withdrew a piece of paper from his pocket—a reprieve from then Governor John Hancock. Hancock eventually pardoned him. I descend from a child he fathered after his near-hanging."[xxxiii]

Completely out of hanging stories to tell, my time had come to end. Watching the faces of my audience, who now looked to Jules and Neil for another story, I knew the truth—if there had been a story-telling vote, it would have unanimous—the stories of Jules and Neil would have won hands down. They were telling their own adventures, not those of their kids or dead ancestors.

Prior to Hurricane Irene, I didn't really know my new Mystic acquaintances, but through our story telling—some exciting while others sad—for we also discussed lost jobs, marriages, children and health—we were becoming friends.

At least I thought so, until another dinner guest, Kristin, told me that if I ever wanted to take the improvisation class she was teaching, I would have to sign a paper stating, "I will try not to be the center of attention."

Gary, too, complained a little about me. When he read my account of his and Cindy's Hurricane Irene rotting meat potlucks, he said to me, "I would never serve rotting meat to my guests. Can't you just say it was defrosted?"

After I explained that no one would want to read about defrosted meat parties, he eventually he came around. (Well, not really, but he resigned himself to the small, but unavoidable cost of befriending a writer.)

There was one person at those potlucks however, Fran, who didn't mind at all when I used her life as a means to move the story along. Yet when I wrote her account of what and how she fed her lizard and snake, some readers complained it was too graphic, so I deleted it. I just can't win! (Come on, aren't you a little curious what's in those packages "discreetly" delivered to Fran's apartment? Especially the ones marked "Frozen Meat"?)

On the sixth day after Hurricane Irene hit, the electricity came back on. It was with some sadness that we all returned to our homes to resume our regular lives. After washing my hair, I went back to my frustrating search for an epic adventure. When was I ever going to find one—or a dead body—of my own?

Neil assured me I never wanted to find a dead body, especially one that had been in the water for a while, but still, I needed something exiting to happen to me.

Little did I know that at our Hurricane Irene rotting food fests, an ember had begun smoldering that would ignite my first real adventure—my first real shot at becoming thin and famous.

Jules and Neil were considering purchasing a sail boat. Listening to my stories that revealed I was an adventurer-wanna-be, they realized they could use that to their advantage…

10 WONDER #8 CONTROVERSY, GLORIA THE GOOSE, EMILY THE CAT, AND BAILEY THE PUBLICITY HOUND

With the publishing of "The 7 Wonders" on the website of the Greater Mystic Chamber of Commerce came the inevitable complaints from the community regarding why I didn't choose their favorite spot. I was particularly scolded for not choosing the Mystic & Noank Library—where the very soul of Mystic finds respite and the ghost of Emily the Cat still roams.

The Mystic & Noank Library was built in an eclectic mix of Italianate and Romanesque styles by Captain Elihu Spicer, a wealthy sea captain and Noank native. Because he wanted it to reflect some of the interesting things he'd seen on his voyages, he chose materials such as Italian tile mosaics and Numidian (huh?) marble from Africa. The library is crowned by gables with one-of-a-kind terracotta reliefs—medallions of Roman deities Minerva, goddess of wisdom and science, and Apollo, god of the arts.

That Apollo and Minerva, with their heads popping out of the roof, were beginning to frighten me. I used to think they were looking out to sea watching for the safe return of ships, but once they heard their library hadn't been chosen, I could swear they were looking down at me—and plotting.

Did the ancient Greek historians have this much trouble when they declared "The Seven Wonders of the World"? No one was stopping Mystic from having eight wonders, why would I?

Bailey and I would have loved to include the library, which offered him treats and me knowledge, but I had also considered choosing the Mystic River Railroad Bridge. I walked Bailey there often to watch it swing open and shut. Just before opening for boats, the bridge makes a scary, electrical sound—just like the sound of the charge Frankenstein gets in old movies. Once the boats get through, the bridge moves so slowly when swinging shut you fear for the oncoming train—wondering if it will close in time.

And what about Gloria, the regal, yet cranky, arthritic goose who had been reigning for more than 20 years over the Olde Mistick Village duck pond? I had discovered this "wonder" goose while interviewing the office manager of Olde Mistick Village.

I figured if the public only knew about Gloria, they would demand the creation of a state-of-the-art exhibit for this feisty goose and highlight me as the writer who discovered her.

Gloria first came to Olde Mistick Village in the mid-1980s when her owner could no longer care for her. Knowing the Village maintained duck ponds for their shoppers to enjoy, her owner thought Gloria could live out her life among the ducks who were permanent residents there. A goose in captivity can live up to 40 years.

Christine Robertson, Office Manager of Olde Mistick Village, said that in early 2010, "an employee of The Gray Goose Cookery told us that Gloria was ailing. She looked a little sluggish to them. She wasn't her normal, feisty self."

Robertson called on a vet in hopes of making Gloria better. She said, "These birds are part of our family, and Gloria is the reigning bird. We call her Queen Gloria because she is very bossy and hisses when displeased— but she is protective of her subjects—especially the swan we once had named Gracie. They were good friends. If a duck or person got too close to the swan, Gloria would warn them off with a hiss."

The vet, who didn't know for sure if Gloria was a female, discovered that she had an infection. So every day, the maintenance man in charge of feeding the birds caught Gloria and held her close to his chest so Robertson could give her an injection. Robertson said, "She started feeling better after the first day, so catching her for the rest of the treatment was almost impossible!" Gloria recovered completely, and despite her arthritis and a slight limp, was still reigning as queen in the main duck pond.

The following winter, while shopping at The Gray Goose Cookery in Olde Mistick Village with Jim and our daughter Jackie who came to Mystic for a visit, I saw a photo of Gloria on a sign beside the cash register. The sign said she had gotten sick again, and this time, the management of the Village was reaching out to the public for donations toward her vet bill.

Gloria's problem? Deciding to take her to a veterinarian who specializes in birds to address her gimpy leg and arthritis, Christine Robertson was in for a big surprise. Gloria was a male—and a very lonely one at that.

The vet thought the key to Gloria's happiness (his name will not be changed) was not only a special diet to help his arthritis, but a female goose—Lulu. "It's become a great love affair," Robertson declared enthusiastically. Then, catching herself, she admitted, "Well, I guess that's an overstatement, but they are learning to tolerate each other!"

Spring is a particularly busy time at the Village because of mating season. Ducks fly in to raise their ducklings, then fly off again. Many, however, live at the Village year-round. Robertson said, "Why would they want to leave? They have everything they need here." The ducks are fed five 50-pound bags of duck food per week by the maintenance crew.[xxxiv]

What happens if age eventually gets the better of Gloria? Robertson said, "We have a duck pond near the maintenance barn that we call the 'Geriatric Ward.' That is where we retire all the birds that are too old or feeble to defend themselves from an aggressive duck." (A plaque memorializing Gloria's swan friend, Gracie, was placed there.)

Bailey and I thought we should pay a visit to Gloria and Lulu and decide for ourselves if a love affair was blossoming between the two. Sitting protectively on her nest of unfertilized eggs, Lulu gave Bailey a good hiss when he approached. Gloria, nearby at the moment, concurred with Lulu's opinion of Bailey, and gave him a hiss too. The ducks, on the other hand, didn't mind Bailey at all—they seemed to feel safe as long as Gloria was around. As Bailey wagged his tail in curiosity at them, the ducks happily paddled around, mated, or watched their fluffy, little ducklings explore the pond, complete with a water wheel and sunken rowboat. Although I'd heard there were moments of terror when a seagull dove down to grab the smallest of the ducklings, this otherwise safe little community of ducks was continuing on as Gloria's obedient subjects.

When I e-mailed Robertson recently for a Duck Chronicle update, she replied with some happy news. "Gloria is doing fine for an old girl. (Sorry, we'll always refer to him as "she"—it's tradition.) She and Lulu are never far from each other these days, and are good companions. When Gloria passes away, we'll find another goose friend for Lulu. It's interesting that we are all such social creatures and don't do well without a friend (or flock). And it's so very touching how people cared so much about Gloria's situation that they wanted to help us care for her."

Although irrational, I felt Gloria deserved to be considered a wonder. I felt just as strongly about her as residents felt about the Mystic & Noank Library and other sites that cause an emotional reaction. Based on a similar response to my article, "The 7 Wonders of Rockland County" (published in *Rockland Magazine*), I had already planned to ask the local media to help me conduct a vote for the "8th Wonder."

Stonington-Mystic Patch agreed to run the online poll: "Cast Your Vote For The Eighth Wonder Of Mystic," with my plea: "With the help of the Greater Mystic Chamber of Commerce and local residents I created a list of '7 Wonders of Mystic.' Now I need your help to determine the 8th Wonder." My article concluded with Patch's call to action: "Vote in our poll and tell us what you think deserves to be the '8th Wonder of Mystic.'"

Although Gloria the goose was initially in the lead, residents urged their neighbors to vote for their library with its stained glass windows, comfy window seat overlooking the valley, ceiling shaped like an upside-down hull, and the scrap book of Emily the Library Cat, which is kept next to the ongoing group puzzle. Although Emily died several years ago, librarians still love to tell visitors about the resident cat who waited by the elevator for patrons so she could catch a ride to the next floor. A guardian of the night, Emily also kept the library bat and cricket populations at bay. Emily is still nearby, but the crickets can chirp happily once again because she is sleeping harmlessly under a bush on the library's property. Her little grave marker is etched with four paw prints and "Emily, 1989-2006." I couldn't help but notice those were the exact years etched in our daughter Elizabeth's stone, giving me another place to visit my happy memories of her.

In the end, the Mystic & Noank Library was overwhelmingly voted the 8th Wonder. The Mystic residents and Roman gods, Apollo and Minerva, were happy once again. The homes along Captains' Row and Gloria the Goose tied for second, Mystic Waterfront Views and Railroad Swing Bridge tied for third, Denison Homestead Museum (built in 1717 and continuously owned by the same family for three centuries) and Mystic River's Art Trail (my term for the art galleries located between the Maritime Gallery at Mystic Seaport and the Mystic Arts Center) tied for fourth.[xxxv] There were several other sites suggested in comments, such as Clancy, the paraplegic dog who pulled himself around town in a little cart.[xxxvi]

After the kerfuffle over the wonders finally died down, there was another controversy in Mystic that just wouldn't go away—what kind of dog was Bailey—really? People often stopped us along our daily walk to ask, "What is he, a basset hound and …"; or "A beagle and…"

While I am his third owner and can't know for sure, his papers from an animal shelter state he is a beagle/basset hound mix. Most are satisfied with that answer. They usually say something like, "Oh yea, I see it now!" But others aren't so sure. "His head looks like a lab's" or "His ears look too small." Nancy, a Mystic local with several pets, doesn't believe he has any beagle in him at all. "If he's part beagle, then he's a beagle on steroids. His personality is that of a large hound, such as an English Fox Hound."

When my friend Heather saw him for the first time, she started to laugh. Considering his long, tank-like body and disproportionately small head, ears and legs, she said, "It looks like God decided to have fun and just took parts from an assortment of dog breeds to see what He could come up with."

Others simply say, "He's funny looking."

His "funny" look is what endeared him to Jim and me—convincing us that we needed him. Some would say we "rescued" him, but that's not how I see it.

Within hours of having our previous dog, Riley, put to sleep because he was terminally ill and suffering, Jackie went online from her college dorm room to find us a new pet. Riley had been Elizabeth's faithful couch companion for the last five years of her life. (Riley was an older dog who came to our family under very unusual circumstances. His and Elizabeth's story is told in my memoir, *Anything But a Dog! The perfect pet for a girl with congenital CMV*).[xxxvii]

With the death of Riley, we felt like Elizabeth died all over again. He was our daily connection to her and now even that was gone. Riley's collar had barely cooled when Jackie called. "Mom, it's not that I don't miss Riley, but I just found a dog on Craigslist that needs a home."

Two days later, Jim and I drove to upstate New York to meet Bailey. When his mistress, a single mother with four cats, opened the door of his large crate kept on the kitchen floor, he exploded out, jumping and scratching us all over with his long basset nails. The moment he caught sight of a cat, he was off—his short basset hound legs, perhaps made a little taller because of his beagle heritage, were no obstacle. In one giant, graceful leap he was over the sofa and on the trail of the poor, harried feline.

His mistress said, "I feel so bad trying to find another home for him, but I just can't control him around my cats—they are my true babies. I got him at the pound when he was about a year old. I had gone in for another cat, but I just couldn't resist that face."

So, this was a dog that was too much for his owners—twice. Jim and I looked at each other grimly, imagining the disruption this hound would be to our quiet home. "But," I whispered to Jim, "he does make me laugh—we could use some of that."

When the owner timidly asked, "Well, what do you want to do about my dog?"

I said, "We'll take him."

Although Bailey was every bit as pesky in our home as we feared, unlike our over-protective Riley, we did not need to muzzle him in public, which vastly improved my social life. Instead of a muzzle, I dressed Bailey in all sorts of friendly bandanas, which has become his trademark.

When Bailey and I strolled through Mystic, tourists frequently asked if they could photograph their children beside Bailey (they never wanted me in the shot). A photographer shooting a wedding party on the Mystic River drawbridge even asked if he could use Bailey as a prop. His face even attracted a Mystic filmmaker who used him in an online dog walking commercial shot in the Mystic River Park. [xxxviii]

Although some called Bailey a "rescue" because we took in an unwanted dog, in truth, Bailey is a "rescue dog" because he rescued me from the overwhelming sadness of losing our daughter and her dog Riley.

Now, if only my rescue hound could rescue me from obscurity!

11 AMELIA EARHART WAS MARRIED HERE—A "DEEP, DARK SECRET"

Learning that *Hope Springs*, the Meryl Streep movie to be filmed in the Mystic area, would hold a casting call for extras in August 2011, I just had to do something to get down to a weight I could declare on the application form.

Perhaps I could kill two birds with one stone—lose weight *and* find an epic adventure by walking the entire Mystic Seafarer's Trail I designed between Stonington to Noank. With only a few days left to the open casting call, I embarked from home on Friday, August 5, 2011, to walk the 2.5 miles to Noank, a quaint little fishing village. (I hoped to lose 20 pounds in that five-mile round trip.)

Bailey and I left our house on Allyn Street and walked straight down to West Mystic Avenue. Passing the former house of Captain Charles Sisson, we made a right on Noank Road, where a sidewalk made for an easy stroll to Noank. I met my seafaring acupuncturist friend Kate there so I could film her in front of the Ford's Lobster shack (seen in the movie, *Mystic Pizza*) where she weighed her baby after giving birth on a schooner on September 15, 1984, and rowing to shore.[xxxix] Kate said that after the lobster scale was cleaned, Araminta was placed on it and weighed in at over eight pounds.

When I was done filming Kate, she and I walked over to the Noank Historical Society's Latham/Chester Store, located between a public beach and an oyster farming business. Kate filmed me in front of the plaque attached to the Latham/Chester Store that states, "Aviation Pioneer Amelia Earhart married George P. Putnam here in Noank, Connecticut, February 7, 1931." I assumed that the words, "here in Noank," meant that she got married in that building, so that is what I said on the video I uploaded to YouTube that very day.

Months later, while eating my breakfast at Carson's Variety Store, a tiny spot where Noank locals have been gathering for a century, I asked the woman sipping her coffee on the stool next to mine what she knew about Earhart's wedding at the Latham/Chester Store.

To my horror, she replied, "She didn't get married there, she got married around the corner on Church Street, in the house that once belonged to my great-grandfather, John McDonald. I don't know what happened with the property after he died on July 17, 1911. I am assuming my great-grandmother lived there until her death. At the time of Amelia Earhart's wedding, it belonged to George Putnam's mother."

Mary Anderson, Curator of the Noank Historical Society, confirmed what my breakfast companion Barbara Servidio told me—that Earhart was indeed secretly married in a simple civil ceremony in the square, flat-roofed house I found on Church Street. (A deed I found at Groton Town Hall confirmed that Mrs. Putnam purchased the house from the estate of Barbara's great-grandfather in 1930.)

Learning I was including this information in a book about the area, Mary said, "You tell everybody that the wedding scene portrayed in the movie [*Amelia*] is inaccurate. My husband's grandfather, the Groton probate judge, performed the ceremony, and my father-in-law, Robert Anderson, a young Noank lawyer at the time, attended as a witness. Before and after the ceremony, Amelia spoke to him about a new kind of aircraft she was promoting. When the judge congratulated her after the ceremony, calling her Mrs. Putnam, she replied, 'Please sir, I prefer Miss Earhart.'"

Most accounts of Earhart's life barely mention her wedding at all, except to say she got married—reluctantly. The 2009 movie *Amelia* starring Hilary

Swank showed her getting married outside—despite the early February date.

I was determined to learn the truth behind this historic event. Mary's comment about Earhart rejecting the name, "Mrs. Putnam," was quickly confirmed. When *The New York Times* announced her wedding the following day, its front-page headline read:

Amelia Earhart Weds G.P. Putnam
But Atlantic Flier Will Remain 'Miss Earhart' for Business Purposes and Writing

To get a better idea of what Noank residents and two black cats experienced the day of the wedding, Mary walked me over to a wide, low cabinet under a display case at the Historical Society's Sylvan Street Museum. Pulling out the drawer containing E's, she handed me the Earhart file full of old newspaper clippings and eye-witness accounts of the secret wedding. This folder was a goldmine—especially the manuscript, "Amelia Earhart in Noank," written by Mary's husband, Noank Attorney Robert Anderson, Jr.

Robert Anderson, Jr., stated in his manuscript that his family became involved with the Putnams when George Putnam's widowed mother, Frances B. Putnam, was looking to buy a summer home near her friend, artist Katherine "Speedy" Forest, in Noank. "My father, then 24 years old and one year out of law school, represented her in the purchase negotiations...To the best of my knowledge she hired him because he was then the only lawyer in Noank."[xl]

When Frances Putnam tried to help her son arrange a private wedding to Amelia in Noank, she contacted the lawyer who handled the purchase of her house. Robert Anderson, Jr., stated, "In preparation for her son's hoped-for marriage to Amelia, Mrs. Putnam asked my father to arrange for a Justice-of-the Peace to perform a small, private ceremony in her home. Not being one to miss such an opportunity, my father volunteered his father, Arthur P. Anderson, who was Groton's Judge of Probate and as such could perform the marriage."

According to the history books, Earhart, originally from Atchison, Kansas, was a "reluctant bride," having refused Putnam's marriage proposals six times. She met Putnam, an arctic explorer, publicist and heir to the GP Putnam publishing company, in 1928 while employed as a social worker in Boston. George Putnam had become famous as the publisher of Charles Lindbergh's book about his solo flight across the Atlantic in 1927. Now George Putnam was helping sponsors look for a woman to become the first woman to fly the Atlantic in the trimotor Fokker, *Friendship*, previously owned by pioneering aviator and polar explorer, Richard E. Byrd. Amelia was interviewed by the flight sponsors in New York City at the offices of G.P. Putnam's Sons Publishing Company. Upon concluding the interview in George Putnam's office, George accompanied Amelia to the train station. Shortly after returning to Boston, she received the offer to make the historic flight.

Although Earhart didn't touch the controls in her transatlantic flight with two male pilots in 1928, she nonetheless received a ticker tape parade in New York as the first woman to make it across the Atlantic by air. She found it embarrassing to receive so much fanfare when she said she felt about as useful as a sack of potatoes on the trip.

Despite her feelings about her role on that flight, she moved into George Putnam's home in Rye, New York, and wrote a book about her experiences. In the process, she became a close friend of George's wife, Dorothy, and their two sons, George Jr. and David. After her book, *20 Hours 40 Minutes*, was completed, Amelia dedicated it to her friend Dorothy Binney Putnam.

In December of 1929, Dorothy divorced George Putnam in Reno, Nevada, citing "failure to provide" and remarried the following month (she would remarry two more times).[xli]

Putnam, who was reportedly smitten by Amelia, brought Earhart to Noank to visit with his mother, Frances Putnam, and on November 8, 1930, he convinced Amelia to visit Groton Town Hall to apply for a marriage license.

Wanting to follow Amelia's trail, I visited Groton Town Hall to see if I could learn anything from looking at the license. Just before I entered the building, a friendly, owner-less golden retriever greeted me. Calling the phone number etched in his tag, I assured the owner I would hold onto him until she could drive over to collect him.

As I sat on a bench with the dog at the entrance of the 1908 brick building, I pondered what Earhart was thinking before she stepped through that doorway more than 80 years earlier. My first trip to Groton Town Hall occurred two years ago when we first moved to Mystic. It wasn't for any life-altering reason—I was just required by law to register Bailey for a Connecticut dog license.

Amelia, on the other hand, was apparently extremely apprehensive when she entered Groton Town Hall. She wasn't sold on the idea of marriage in general (her parents had divorced six years earlier in 1924) [xlii] and had rejected other marriage proposals, including Sam Chapman's, whose proposal included the insistence that his wife not work outside the home.

According to Amelia's friends, she felt an additional reluctance to marry George Putnam because she had become friends with his first wife, Dorothy. According to author Susan Butler, Earhart was unhappy to think Putnam's feelings for her were a cause of their divorce.[xliii] Although Dorothy was already remarried, her divorce from Putnam was less than a year old.

Once freed from my dog sitting responsibilities, I visited the Registrar of Vital Statistics office, the same office where I applied for Bailey's dog license.

When I told the clerk I was looking for Earhart's marriage license and gave her the wedding date, she found it immediately. "We've had many requests for that," she said. She handed me the book containing the original license so I could decide if I wanted to pay the $20 for a certified copy of it. I touched Amelia's signature, hoping that some of her adventurous spirit would rub off on me. Wanting extra insurance that it would, I purchased a certified, first generation copy of it with a raised seal. Now I had certified proof that Amelia could tell a lie—she listed herself as 32, a year younger than she really was at 33. According to authors Elgen M. and Marie K. Long, this deception began on a May 1923 aviator pilot certificate that stated she was born on July 24, 1898.[xliv] She was actually born on July 24, 1897. For whatever reason, she continued to give the public, including Groton Town Hall, that younger age.

At the time Earhart and Putnam applied for the wedding license, Connecticut law required a five-day waiting period from the application to the wedding. On the back of the marriage license, a typed statement from Probate Court was attached (misspelling Earhart's last name, a handwritten "a" was inserted after the "e") granting the couple permission to celebrate the intended marriage "without delay." Nevertheless, Earhart did delay.

William, the youngest son of Probate Judge Arthur Anderson, recalled his impression of the reluctant bride in a 1989 article by Larry Chick: "*Amelia and George came to see my father at his house at the corner of Brook and Elm. They wanted to talk to him about the possibility of his marrying them, and I was the teenager in the way who was shooed into another room to give them some privacy. But even in the next room I heard her ask my father if she could go into his study and have a cigarette and think about marriage. When she came out, she had decided against it.*"[xlv]

According to the 2009 *Amelia* movie and other sources, Earhart didn't smoke and was criticized for promoting Lucky Strike cigarettes on her first trip across the Atlantic (smoking wasn't considered ladylike). Isn't it just like a little brother to tell on you for smoking—whether you did or not?

Promoting cigarettes gave Earhart a continued connection to Rear-Admiral Richard E. Byrd, the polar explorer who previously owned the Fokker she used on her first transatlantic flight. Byrd had also come to the Mystic area when he visited the Nathanial B. Palmer House in Stonington to study Palmer's notes on the Antarctic in preparation for his history-making flight over the South Pole on November 29, 1929. (According to Mary Beth Baker, Director of the Stonington Historical Society, "He [Byrd] wanted to review the logbooks, journals, charts, and letters that had accumulated over the years in the family home." According to research by

Palmer House's first curator, Constance Colom, "It was at Byrd's suggestion that the family donated *Hero's* logbook to the Library of Congress in the 1930s."[xlvi])

Earhart had gotten to know Byrd and his wife in Boston while preparing for her flight across the Atlantic in his former plane.[xlvii] Byrd served as a technical consultant for the trip.[xlviii] Less than two months after her successful flight, Earhart contributed financially to Byrd's flight over the South Pole. On July 30, 1928, she sent a letter to Byrd at the Biltmore Hotel in New York (letter online at Ohio State University Libraries) stating, *"Perhaps you noticed my 'endorsement' of a kind of cigarettes which were carried by the men in the plane. I made this deliberately. It made possible my offering a modest contribution to your Antarctic expedition, which otherwise I could not have done."*[xlix]

When Earhart supposedly smoked a cigarette in Judge Anderson's study and came out deciding against marriage for the moment, Robert Anderson recalled her mood in a 1976 article by reporter Jeff Mill. *"Amelia was a little bit subdued. She just wanted to think about the whole thing more. She had dedicated herself to the business of flying, and she was anxious to retain her individuality. She was very devoted to George, there's no doubt about that. But she was afraid that changing her name somehow would diminish her stature, and she was a little upset about it."* Robert added that George Putnam *"was very considerate about it."*[l]

When the media learned that no wedding occurred upon taking out the wedding license, it fell to Robert Anderson, as Mrs. Putnam's lawyer and friend, to tell reporters that the wedding had been delayed, not cancelled.

Three months later, on Friday, February 6, 1931, George Putnam called his mother and told her he and Amelia would be secretly driving out from New York to Noank that night. They would marry the following day, February 7 (the *Titanic* couple I featured earlier, the Smiths, also got married on a February 7—perhaps this is not a good wedding date for those planning a trip across an ocean?).

Very few knew that Earhart and Putnam had come to Noank, but resident Clifford Sullivan, approximately 12 at the time, stated in the 1976 Mill article that when he heard the news that "Lady Lindy" was in town, it was *"like trying to get into the Kennedy compound in Hyannis..."* He and his friends rode up and down the street on their bicycles, *"trying to get a peek of, you know, Amelia Earhart."*[li]

When reporters caught wind of what was going on, Robert Anderson's younger brother Ashby got his chance to participate in the historic event. Repeatedly calling the judge's home, the reporters wanted details on the couple's plans. According to the article by Chick, Ashby and his brothers avoided giving them any answers by telling them they had to call the judge's secretary to get that kind of information.[lii]

On the day of the wedding, Putnam received a typed letter, or some would say contract, from Amelia. I read a copy of her handwritten draft (available online at Purdue University Libraries), which is just slightly different than the typed one he received (the handwritten draft was done on stationery I presume was Mrs. Putnam's, and included cross-outs and insertions as Amelia fine-tuned what she wanted to say). The stationary didn't have an exact address for George Putnam's home, but it was printed with the following in all capitals:

PHONE MYSTIC 1016
TELEPHONE NOANK
NOANK, CONNECTICUT
THE SQUARE HOUSE
CHURCH STREET

The following are excerpts from Amelia's handwritten version:
...You must know again my reluctance to marry, my feeling that I shatter thereby chances in work which means most to me...
On our life together I want you to understand I shall not hold you to any midaevil [Earhart's misspelling, not mine!] *code of faithfulness to me nor shall I consider myself so bound to you. If we can be honest about affection for others which may come to* [either] *of us the difficulties of such situations may be avoided...*
I must exact a cruel promise and that is you will let me go in a year if we find no happiness together...[liii]

Just prior to the noon wedding, Amelia sat speaking to Robert Anderson, who was serving as a witness, on a couch in a small sitting room in the back of the yellow house. There were no special wedding decorations, not even flowers.
"She was completely wrapped up in the aviation business," Anderson said.[liv] The groom, his mother, and his uncle, were also in the room.
Amelia told Robert about her desire to interest the Army and Navy in the military potential of the autogyro, a precursor to the helicopter. Robert Anderson, Jr., recalled what his father told him about that conversation: "Although the Navy representatives were considerably more receptive than their Army counterparts, you can just imagine how unwelcome this advice was to the generals and admirals she visited, and she was treated accordingly. Even at her wedding she was still steaming at their repudiation of her. Pa let her talk, just to get the anger out of her system. But no such thing. My grandfather and George summoned Amelia to step forward for the five-minute ceremony (totally secular and omitting all mention of "obedience"), and almost reluctantly she went over to be married."[lv]
The men wore business attire and Amelia wore a brown traveling suit, light brown blouse, shoes and stockings. Robert Anderson said that she was *"a much more attractive individual as a young woman than she was depicted...she was*

61

quite delicate looking with beautiful color and light brown hair—all in all, very attractive." Robert recalled that it was *"quite obvious that she had become satisfied that she did want to go through with it* [the wedding]."[lvi]

Although *The New York Times* stated that the ceremony took place in the living room while a "crackling fire burned in the fireplace," Robert Anderson remembered that his father (the judge) stood in the dining room, Earhart and Putnam stood in the passageway between the sitting room and dining room, and behind them stood George's mother and himself. Wherever the ceremony took place, all agree it was over in less than five minutes. Robert said, *"They both wanted it that way, so my father did little more than bring out the essentials of the marriage contract.'*[lvii]

The New York Times added: "*As Mr. Putnam slipped a plain platinum ring on Miss Earhart's finger the cats, coal black and playful, rubbed arched backs against his ankles.*"[lviii]

After the ceremony, Earhart and Robert returned to the sofa. Where, according to Robert Anderson, Jr., Amelia "resumed her diatribe against those stuffed shirts in the War Department."

George's mother came over to them, placed a set of amber beads around Amelia's neck and leaned down to kiss her.[lix] Preparing to leave, Judge Anderson came forward to congratulate everyone, addressing Amelia as "Mrs. Putnam."

Amelia replied, "Please, sir, I prefer Miss Earhart."

According to Robert Anderson, Jr. during our phone interview, his grandfather was unaccustomed to such "modern" airs. "My grandfather drew himself up to his full 5 feet, 8 inches, and barked, 'That service was short but effective.'"[lx] With that, he left.

George Putnam called his secretary in New York to announce the wedding. There was no reception or honeymoon, and the couple was back at their desks on Monday.

The New York Times described Noank as a "quaint little village," one that "dozes" in the winter. In regard to the wedding, most of the residents were "asleep," having no idea what had just taken place. One recalled the event as a "deep, dark secret."[lxi]

Another said, "It was all very hush-hush. I don't think the people next-door even knew about it."[lxii]

According to comments from Noank's Historian, Mary Virginia Goodman, residents "wouldn't go all to pieces about this sort of thing" and described the couple as "outlanders invading our little village."[lxiii] Despite Goodman's opinion of the "outlanders," she did accommodate the request made by phone to her home the following day. She was asked if she could provide a picture of the house where Earhart had married and send it to a business in New York that sold photographs to newspapers. To fulfill this assignment, Goodman said she "obtained the services of Moses W.

Rathbun, the village postmaster at the time, who was also very good with a camera..." Goodman took the roll of film, along with a photograph of Judge Anderson, which he provided, and rode the trolley to New London, Connecticut. From there, she sent the images by express to New York.[lxiv]

When interviewed by the *New York Times* about the wedding shortly afterwards, George's mother confirmed there had been no fuss, no flowers, and the neighbors had not been notified. When the subject of flying came up, she said she had never been, and although she was afraid, she intended to fly with her daughter-in-law soon. Amelia had promised her, "I'll take you for a ride the next time I come up here."

"I'll not be afraid with her," Frances Putnam told the interviewer.[lxv]

Apparently, Earhart was happy enough in her marriage to Putnam. That Christmas, they sent Judge Anderson a card with a caricature of themselves flying together in an autogyro, which, in the sketch, looks like a small, open cockpit airplane with a propeller attached to its nose and a large one on top. A giant Santa is holding the autogyro in the air. Underneath Santa, it states:

Happy Landings!
G.P.P
A.E.[lxvi]

Putnam and Earhart continued to plan and promote her flying projects after their marriage. A few months after the wedding, Amelia set a world altitude record in an autogyro;[lxvii] and in 1932, she became the first woman to fly solo nonstop across the Atlantic—a trip fraught with weather and mechanical problems. Her Lockheed Vega even went into a spin, sending her toward "whitecaps too close for comfort."[lxviii]

In 1936, Earhart began planning a round-the-world flight, intending to take the long, dangerous route near the equator—despite the fact that several pilots had died in the attempt. Earhart's last, legendary flight occurred in a specially modified Lockheed Electra 10E, which she dubbed the "flying laboratory."

On July 2, 1937, Earhart and her navigator, Fred Noonan, disappeared somewhere over the Pacific Ocean. They were unable to find Howland Island, where they were scheduled to land for refueling. Among her last words reported to the Coast Guard cutter, *Itasca*, were: "We must be on you, but cannot see you—but gas is running low. Have been unable to reach you by radio. We are flying at 1,000 feet."

After an extensive, expensive search failed to find Earhart, Noonan, and the Lockheed Electra, the government abandoned its search on July 18. George Putnam financed his own search until October 1937.[lxix]

Putnam publicly released a letter Earhart had given him in the event one of her flights ended in tragedy: *"Please know that I am quite aware of the hazards.*

I want to do it—because I want to do it. Women must try to do things as men have tried. When they fail, their failure must be but a challenge to others.[lxx]

A year and a half after her disappearance, on January 5, 1939, Putnam had her declared legally dead—way ahead of the required seven-year waiting period. He remarried that same year, but was divorced in 1944, and remarried again. He died January 4, 1950, in California.

The home Earhart and Putnam were married in is now a privately owned duplex. According to a 1979 article by reporter Steve Fagin, the owner celebrated her wedding anniversary annually with his friends. In her honor, they've raised their glasses to her and sung, "For She's a Jolly Good Fellow."[lxxi]

In June of 2010, NavList, a community of celestial navigation enthusiasts, wanted the public to know that Earhart had a very personal connection to Noank so donated the sign I found attached to the Noank Historical Society's Latham/Chester Store. Frank Reed, manager of NavList, believed Earhart's flying companion, Fred Noonan, was a top navigator. In a 2010 article by Matt Collette, Reed said, "[Noonan] *was the sort of person who knew how to get across oceans precisely, accurately...But a few clouds could ruin their day, and that's very well what could have happened."*[lxxii]

Although most of the world believes Amelia simply ran out of fuel over the Pacific Ocean near Howland Island, the possibility that her plane landed on a reef off the remote Pacific island of Nikumaroro is currently under investigation by The International Group for Historic Airplane Recovery (TIGHAR). A statement from their website: *"A review of high-definition underwater video footage taken during the recently-completed Niku VII expedition has revealed a scattering of man-made objects on the reef slope off the west end of Nikumaroro. The newly discovered debris field is in deep water offshore the location where an object thought to be Lockheed Electra landing gear appears in a photo taken three months after Amelia Earhart disappeared. Items in the debris field appear to be consistent with the object in the 1937 photo."*[lxxiii]

In 1940, a partial skeleton of a woman matching Earhart's size and race, plus a jar the shape of an anti-freckle cream available in the 30s, was found in the remains of a campfire under a tree on the island of Nikumaroro (Earhart was known to dislike her freckles). Had Earhart used that jar to boil water? The heel and partial sole of a woman's shoe manufactured in the 1930s, plus a box used to hold a nautical sextant (a navigational tool) were also found. Did Earhart and Noonan die as castaways? If so, how long did they struggle to stay alive, hoping for rescue?

In a 2012 article by Malia Mattoch McManus, fish and bird bones were also found[lxxiv] suggesting someone might have been marooned for months.

(Note to self: If I ever find a friend with a sailboat, I must learn celestial navigation, how to use a GPS—and how to catch fish!)

12 HOLLYWOOD, HERE I COME!

The day, August 11, 2011, had finally arrived—the casting call for *Hope Springs*. The announcement said I was to bring a head shot and a resume. Having gained weight walking the seafarer's trail from all the fried clam strips, pizza and ice-cream I found along the way, I would also have to bring, or rather wear, something else—a girdle.

I had missed the casting call at the Stonington High School so had to drive with my kayak friend Cindy to a hotel in New Haven, where they offered a second chance.

Just going to New Haven, a place I had never been before, was exciting. I got to see where thousands played extras in the film, *Indiana Jones and the Crystal Skull*, which featured a chase scene all over the Yale University campus. I also got to see where traitor Benedict Arnold's first wife was buried in the basement of a church.

When we reached the hotel where the casting call was held, we were ushered into a meeting room where I was handed a form to fill out. Oh no—it wanted to know my weight. I knew I should tell the truth, so I wrestled with the question for a few moments before coming to the conclusion that I should give them the weight I planned to be in September when shooting was scheduled to begin. They also wanted to know if I had any "props" I could bring—like a dog.

Did I have a dog! Gosh, why didn't I bring his headshot, featuring his saggy, "please pick me" eyes? I never thought of that. The form also wanted to know what kind of car I drove and if I had a bicycle. Bicycle? Hoping that Mystic Community Bikes would lend me one of theirs, I checked yes. Cindy said I could also add on the form that I had access to kayaks since she would lend me hers if necessary.

Handing in the form to a woman manning a table, I bent her ear for a moment trying to embellish my experience. To my horror, they wanted to take my picture holding a piece of paper with my name on it. Now they would know for sure I had fibbed about my weight when they studied my photo against the height and weight I listed on the form. I really was like Amelia Earhart! Although the casting agency form wasn't a legal document like her marriage license (or was it?), they would know the truth about me. And if I ever did become famous, some writer years from now will dredge up that form and point out what I'd done to conceal my true size.

When I looked around at the clothes the other extra hopefuls were wearing, I realized I'd made a big mistake in my wardrobe choice. I wore my fanciest dress in hopes of looking attractive, but the other applicants, the ones who told me they had worked as extras before, looked like they had just come in off the street (or boat)—very casual, very little make-up. Of course! I should have gone in looking like the average person you'd see in a seacoast village—not in the dress I wore to my daughter's New York wedding rehearsal dinner. I was supposed to look like a salty New Englander coming in from a sail, not a fancy New Yorker about to embark on a cocktail party.

Was there a way to overcome my mistake? When I got home, I thought about e-mailing them a video of Bailey and me beside a marina so they would see how nautical we looked together. When I asked my daughter Jackie if I should do it, she was horrified. "Mom, the casting people will think you're a pest or a stalker."

My casino commercial friend Kristin, however, saw my YouTube video and said, "Send the video. They are culling right now by look, and if you happen to make it into that pile, she'll remember you were engaging or crazy, but either way, she'll remember you. And that's good!"

Excerpt of my e-mail to the casting agency:

If you are wondering if my beagle/ basset hound has the right "look" for the film, here is a very short YouTube video of us together in Mystic.[lxxv]

To see him being walked, he played an "extra" in this online dog-walking commercial shot in Mystic (he is the hound on your left).[lxxvi]

...

Sincerely,
Lisa Saunders

I heard nothing back. My hopes of Hollywood were dashed.

Figuring I'd give the *Hope Springs* film crew one more chance, Bailey and I strolled up and down the streets of Stonington on the last morning of the shoot trying to look perfect as a last-minute add in. While I took photos of the set, I absent-mindedly set down my cell phone in Cannon Square, not realizing it until I was back to my car.

Racing back to Cannon Square (which holds the two cannons used to beat back the British in the Battle of Stonington in the War of 1812), I was told by one member of the film crew that another crew member had it. Tracking him down, I hoped he would see in my face, or in Bailey's, how well we represented New England seafarers. But when I approached the man for my phone, all he did was hand it back to me without a serious glance. So ended my glorious film career.

To add to the humiliation of this rejection and dashed hopes, I crossed paths with a woman walking up and down the street with her two large dogs that were off-leash. She was giving them abnormally loud commands, such as "stay," "come," as though she was trying to show the film crew how obedient they were—just in case they needed a dog extra with their handler. The moment the dogs caught sight of Bailey, they disregarded their mistress's commands to "heel" and tried to take advantage of him in ways too degrading to print. Time to go home and leave Hollywood behind.

Before we sped out of Stonington's town parking lot to lick our wounds, however, Bailey and I took one more stroll through the movie crew's trailers, passed the commercial fishing fleet tied to the docks, which included large trawlers for catching scallops and stacks of lobster pots, to visit the Stonington Fishermen's Memorial. I read over the list of fishermen who died at sea and pondered the sad widows and children left behind. I thought of the very old, retired lobster fisherman I had met recently at a party in Mystic, Captain James Arruda Henry. When I asked him if he ever lost someone at sea, he choked up and could barely speak. Yes, he had—his cousin Arthur. "I just couldn't save him," was all he managed to say. He couldn't bear to speak about it, but said I could read the story in his book, *In a Fisherman's Language*. He hadn't learned to read until his 90s, and when he did, he wrote a collection of short stories about his life. His granddaughter Marlisa helped him publish his stories into the book, which I hear, is going to become a movie. Even if I never make it into that film as an extra, I will still be sure to see it.

(Captain Henry passed away at the age of 99 in January 2013. He was working on his second book).

13 CHRISTMAS IN CONNECTICUT. THEN, SHANGHAIED!

Christmas 2011: My second Christmas in Mystic meant another form letter to my friends and family listing all my failed attempts at getting thin and famous. In the fall, when called in for jury duty in New London, I couldn't even get picked by a scary-looking criminal and his lawyer after my courtroom interview. Maybe because I was too eager to be chosen. It's always been a dream of mine to be selected for a highly publicized case, get sequestered with lots of pizza, then sign a book deal with a major publisher.

Still, despite my failures, I was enjoying my second round of Mystic Christmas traditions, such as singing carols with the rest of the community around a 7,000-pound anchor at Mystic Seaport (it had belonged to a British warship and was salvaged off Newport, Rhode Island). Then, Jim and I went to Bambi's house for her annual fish stew dinner, where Edgar, her droopy basset hound, served as the entertainment. As usual, the poor hound was repeatedly banished to his crate because he got caught stealing food off the table. Believe me, I didn't tell on him—it was too amusing to watch guests leave their plates unattended, assuming that Edgar was too short to reach them (Bailey, having a long, basset body, also had a high reach when it came to food). I secured Edgar's crate release over and over, convincing Bambi that his mournful look and pitiful howls meant that he was truly sorry that time.

Later that week, as Bailey and I strolled past the special village mailbox marked "Letters to Santa," I thought of all the hopes expressed by the children who mailed letters to their friend at the North Pole. Answered by the Greater Mystic Chamber of Commerce, I learned that while many contained detailed requests for particular toys, others simply asked for "a job for Daddy."

Christmas is a time when losses, such as the death of our daughter Elizabeth, feel keener.[lxxvii] Despite all my buried hopes that year for finding a new career as a movie star or best-selling author, I did have some good news to share in my annual Christmas letter, such as my play, "Ever True: A Union Private and His Wife," was going to be produced in Mystic for the first time as a Valentine's Day dinner theater,[lxxviii] and the publisher of my book, *Anything But a Dog*, converted it into an e-book, which meant the world could read my first chapter for free online, giving me hope that more babies would be spared from the disabilities Elizabeth faced.

In addition to that, I was filled with renewed optimism that something monumental might happen to me in 2012—that I just might be given what I had been looking for since moving to Mystic. Excerpt of my Christmas form letter:

My friend Jules [blind adventuress] *and her fiancé, Neil* [career Navy], *just bought a sailboat and promised to take Jim and me along on overnight trips to Block Island* [Amelia Earhart went deep-sea diving off that nearby island in 1929]. *I feel especially qualified for an adventure like this because I just learned how to tie a bowline knot, the kind Sherlock Holmes always attributes to sailors when analyzing clues in a case.*

Last week, Jules and Neil gave their first official sailing plans to our friend Kate, asking her to call the Coast Guard if she didn't hear from them by a certain time. Neil let us know that it would be very humiliating for a Navy guy to be rescued by the Coast Guard...

What happened a month later seemed almost too good to be true. On Friday, January 27, 2012, Jim and I were invited by Jules and Neil over for dinner. Prior to arriving at their apartment located near Captain's Row, I asked Jules to serve cheap, box wine with the meal. Jim had been reluctant to try box wine, so I didn't want him to have other options that night. Jules, willing to expand his horizons, agreed.

Tasting something new was about as adventurous as Jim ever hoped to be, and until I got a "real" job with benefits, we needed to learn how to entertain our guests on a smaller budget.

After we'd had a few glasses, Jim was beginning to like the idea of serving cheap wine to his guests. Now, Neil decided, was the time to stretch Jim's newly awakened adventurous side even further.

"Hey Jim," he asked, "how would you like to save even more money by taking a free sailing vacation? I'm taking off work in early March so Jules and I can sail our boat up from the Chesapeake Bay to Mystic—you can come along as our guests."

Sitting all warm and comfy on the couch, Jim's smile froze.

Answering for Jim, I yelled, "You're kidding!"

We were actually getting a shot at a real adventure! I asked, "What will our jobs be? Yell 'Land, ho!'?"

"No need for that. We will always be in sight of land." I felt disappointed—our voyage would be so tame. Now if we were going to be rounding Cape Horn that would be an epic adventure.

At least I would have the fun of yelling "Ahoy there" to anyone relaxing along the shore. Do people relax on the New Jersey Shore in early March?

Suddenly Jim rallied. Remembering his role as the voice of reason, and his frozen toes when seal watching last March, he said, "In March? Isn't the air still really cold over the water that time of year?"

I had to admit, Jim was right to be a little concerned about our role as crew in the winter—especially since we had zero sailing experience between us. Just the night before, I attended a Mystic Seaport "Adventure Series" talk given by a man who sailed to Greenland. His video highlighted an unhappy-looking crew member in a wetsuit jumping into frigid water to scrape barnacles off his hull.

I asked Neil, "Are you going to make us scrape barnacles off your hull?" (I didn't really know what barnacles were, but people in Mystic were always scraping them.)

Neil laughed. "Gosh, no, it's too cold for that."

Recalling how the Greenland sailor also made his crew sleep in the forward cabin where the heat wasn't as good, and the ride was bumpy because waves are hit head-on from there, I asked, "Which cabin will you be giving us?"

Jim, thinking he had learned what a keel was, ventured, "Will we be sleeping on the keel?"

Instead of laughing at Jim this time (he was still trying to sell the idea), Neil said, "No, the keel is the 'backbone' of the boat. You'll be sleeping in the forward cabin, called the V-berth. The mattress is shaped like a V, so it can fit within the shape of the bow."

Seeing that Jim loved learning new seafaring terms, Neil added what happened to sailors who were actually keelhauled. "Keelhauling is a form of punishment. Unruly sailors are tied to a rope, thrown overboard, and dragged underwater from one side of the boat to another. If they don't drown, they will most likely be shredded by the barnacles on the hull."

Since Jim thought sleeping in the front of the boat meant he was being given the cabin of honor, I decided to keep my mouth shut so he'd agree to go. Besides, Jim and I should experience sleeping where all greenhorns have slept throughout the ages.

For the rest of the night, Jules and Neil took turns assuring Jim how safe and fun it would be. The boat would be well heated below deck, they would bring all kinds of hand and foot warmers, and we would go ashore every evening to dine in elegant marina restaurants. We could even bring Bailey along.

Jules and Neil told Jim he could just laze around the salon (fancy way of saying he could sit on a cushioned bench in the main living area), sleep in as late as he wanted, drink cheap, boxed wine and make microwave popcorn all day in their modern galley (kitchen). For emphasis, they showed him a picture of their galley table with a TV mounted above it so he could picture watching his favorite DVDs.

Although depressed that he would miss college basketball's "March Madness" on TV, by the end of the evening Jim could no longer resist—"Hey, why not! I'll go, it sounds fun!"

I couldn't believe it! We were no longer going to be the Mystic newcomers trying to appear nautical with their whale-shaped door knocker and sailing books strewn about their coffee table—we were going to become real sailors! No longer would Jim ask questions like, "What's a keel?" He would know first-hand.

Falling asleep that night, I couldn't believe I was about to embark on an epic adventure of my own. I had read numerous adventure stories from the comfort of my warm bed, thrilled to live vicariously through someone else's bravery and misery. Now it was possible that perfect strangers might read my story of misery and thrills from the comfort of their beds.

But would sailing in early March mean I would suffer more misery than thrills? I could still hear the plunk, plunk, plunk of frozen toes being amputated into a tin can when I read about Earnest Shackleton's misadventure in Antarctica. And what about the original 1930 newspaper I found lining an old, family trunk? I had framed and hung it in our hallway because it headlined famed South Pole explorer Richard E. Byrd: *'BYRD PLIGHT IS REGARDED AS PERILOUS—Lives May Be Lost if Help Fails To Reach Them—HASTE IS IMPERATIVE—Ice Packs Threaten to Isolate Explorers With Food Supplies Running Low."*

Was that a sign of things to come? Common themes in sailing adventure stories are hypothermia, starvation, scurvy (note to self: pack limes), cannibalism and insanity. Were we insane already? Were we about to embark on our own "March Madness?"

When Jim awoke the next morning, the reality of what we were about to do overwhelmed him. He asked, "What did I just agree to do? It's going to be *really* cold. What if I'm seasick? What if I can't sleep on that bed?" Hmm. Jim couldn't even sleep in hotels because it took him a while to get used to a strange bed. The v-shaped bed was going to be strange all right.

Listening to Jim, I wondered if I had witnessed a shanghaiing the previous evening, so I looked up the definition of the word online. According to Oxforddictionaries.com, when someone shanghaies another, it means to "force (someone) to join a ship lacking a full crew by drugging them or using other underhand means."

I *had* witnessed a shanghaiing! And I thought this only happened in the sailing yarns of old. It can happen just as easily today using cheap wine and promises of microwaved popcorn and DVDs!

Enjoying the fact that I had witnessed a shanghaiing first-hand, while I, on the other hand, was more than ready to embark on a swashbuckling adventure, I e-mailed our friends with the exciting news. Knowing Jim's quiet and predictable habits, many felt inspired to respond with all kinds of jokes. Jules, perhaps slightly offended I had accused her of shanghaiing my husband, e-mailed me back with, "He was not forced, but discovered his inner adventure child." (Jules uses words like "inner-child," because when she's not sailing, she's a therapist.)

Kate, my sailor friend who gave birth to her daughter on the schooner, said, "No, no. He was plied with dreams of cheap wine and sleeping in to the restful sound of gentle waves and sweet wind in the rigging. Personally, if I get shanghaied, it would be for cheap rum instead of cheap wine."

My girlfriend Chris said, "I can't see Jim stuffing his belongings into a seaman's bag and go off sailing. I picture him vacationing in places where he can bring his clothes folded neatly into one of those large, rectangular suitcases on wheels. He seems better suited to a hotel where he can unpack his toothbrush and slide it into a ceramic toothbrush holder attached to the wall."

Jim, normally agreeable to his various roles in my story telling, finally had enough. "You're making me look like the wimp in this venture. How do you know you're really up to this? You've never done this before—and it will be cold!"

After reminding him that anyone married to a writer should be willing to sacrifice their dignity a little for the sake of a good story (Jules has noted this goes for friends of writers as well), I e-mailed my friends that Jim was tired of looking like a wimp.

Jules rescued Jim's lost dignity with her reply: "Certainly no wimps were invited on this journey."

The next day, however, all fun banter ceased as Jules and Neil realized they had a lot of work to do to get us ready for the trip. Me knowing how to tie a bowline knot was not enough.

E-mail from Jules to me on Thursday, Feb 2, 2012: *"We ought to study knots and tide charts."*

Tide charts? I thought Jim and I didn't have to do anything on this voyage except keep them company. Just serve as a kind of fun cargo. Why would we need to understand tide charts?

Jules replied:

"Because we need to determine when to arrive at certain places, like the bridge where our main mast will only clear the underside by one and half feet—at low tide. We have to be very certain we are at the lowest tide possible before sailing through. We may need to go

through it at 4 a.m."

What! We had to worry about getting stuck under a bridge-at 4 a.m.?

14 SHANGHAIED PART II

In an effort to make our inland sailing lessons more fun, Jules decided Jim and I should have titles. As the most experienced sailor, Jules would be making all the sailing decisions. Having named their 33' sloop *Watercolors* in honor of her passion for art, she went on to declare herself Sailing Master; Neil, Captain; Jim, Skipper; and me, Navigator. I was pleased with Navigator, especially since I had recently learned how to locate the North Star. No matter what time of night or time of year, it stays in virtually the same position, making it an ideal tool for celestial navigation for those who live in the northern hemisphere (unless, of course, it's a cloudy night).

And yet, maybe I didn't want that title. Although it sounded more impressive than deck-swabber, everyone blames the navigator, not the deck-swabber, when voyages go awry—as in Amelia Earhart's disappearance when her navigator Fred Noonan was unable to locate Howland Island.

To tell the truth, although I *knew* how to find the North Star, actually finding it was a very different matter. For such an important star, the North Star isn't very bright and shiny. Located at the end of the little dipper, you'd think it would be easy to spot, but even the little dipper can be allusive at times (it's near the bowl part of the big dipper). Plus, there would be a whole lot more to learn than the North Star if I really wanted to help with navigation. But did I really need to bother since Jules and Neil had GPS (Global Positioning System), the satellite navigation system?

When I asked a seasoned world sailor why he took the trouble to continually study celestial navigation given the capabilities of GPS, he replied, "Are you kidding me? Every sailor, especially those who travel off shore, should learn celestial navigation. You need battery power to operate a GPS. What if the battery on the boat dies?"

When I wrote to Frank Reed, NavList manager and celestial navigation instructor, about the necessity of learning celestial navigation as a backup for GPS, he wrote back:

Well, as for GPS, I'll tell you what I tell everybody: the best backup for a GPS is another GPS (carefully stowed in a metal case with spare batteries replaced before every trip out of sight of land). Celestial navigation can be a worthwhile "backup of last resort," but it's no replacement for GPS. GPS has many advantages over traditional celestial navigation:

1) GPS is more accurate by a factor of 100. That's enough to steer around local hazards and operate in hazardous waters even with zero visibility. By contrast, celestial navigation only provides a position fix accurate to a mile or two and must be supplemented with other navigational methods when close to shore.

2) GPS provides a nearly continuous position plot. There's no need to extrapolate from your last fix. It's always "live."

3) GPS is easy. A child can understand it in five minutes.

4) GPS can be, and usually is, incorporated into a complete charting solution. The customizable displays of modern GPS "systems" include charts and can include built-in hazard avoidance intelligence and displays of other vessels' positions, too (have you seen marinetraffic.com? It's fun for identifying and tracking larger vessels off southern New England).

5) THE BIG ONE: GPS is all-weather. You can use it in the middle of a hurricane. By contrast, a few clouds or simply a hazy horizon can render celestial navigation useless for days at a time.

Of course, GPS does have some disadvantages, and these require learning and adapting to some modern issues. The biggest issue, of course, is power failure. If a full GPS "system" goes down, you lose many of the advantages I listed above. If you have a backup, handheld GPS, you will know exactly where you are in terms of latitude and longitude, which is great. But where is home? A modern navigator needs a set of latitude/longitude waypoints, written down on some waterproof material that can at least get you back to a safe port by following the readout of a basic handheld GPS. And of course, batteries—lots and lots of batteries, for the backup device.

So why bother with celestial navigation at all? First, there are non-essential reasons that have a lot of merit: it's a mark of a true mariner, it's a link to a great historical tradition of navigation, and it's good, clean fun. For practical navigation, it's one of those things that you might never use in a lifetime, but if that day arrives when all the electronics are out, and someone forgot to buy batteries, but just by chance you remembered to buy the Nautical Almanac for the current year, then the stars can get you across an ocean just as easily as they did 150 years ago. And many mariners still enjoy it because it provides that assurance of independence—the confidence that you won't need to call for help and put someone else's life at risk just because you forgot to buy batteries. From my perspective, that's the best practical reason for learning celestial navigation."

Frank Reed, Conanicut Island, Rhode Island

Knowing celestial navigation was how Mystic's Captain Thomas Wolfe was able to negotiate through enemy territory to the north when he and his comrades escaped from a Confederate prison. Given that we were going to be very close to Confederate territory at the start of our trip in the Chesapeake Bay, I had better take the time to learn celestial navigation—at least some of it.

Although my landlubbing New York friends were excited about my upcoming adventure, my seasoned Mystic sailor friends were alarmed at the time of year we were going. When I told Mary, my neighbor who sailed across the Atlantic a few times, that we were leaving in March, her face fell—very far. Gravely quiet for a moment, she finally managed to say, "I can lend you my foul weather gear...and my harness."

What was a harness, and why would I need one? Why did she look so ill when I gave her my news? I didn't want to ask—I didn't want to know. But, I was beginning to wonder—had I, too, been shanghaied?

When Jules, my sailor friend Kate, and Bailey and I met for coffee at Green Marble Coffee House to discuss our trip, Kate asked Jules, "With the erratic winds in March, you're not tempted to sail through Hell's Gate, are you?"

Alarmed, I asked, "What's Hell's Gate?"

Kate replied, "It's one of the most treacherous passages on the eastern seaboard. It's a tight channel in New York City with a rocky shore in the East River—it's actually a tidal strait connecting three major bodies of water. You can get sucked into a whirlpool or smashed into Execution Rocks if you make a piloting error or misjudge the wind and tide."

At home, I looked up Hell's Gate on the Internet, and found that it's officially called Hell Gate. It has been the site of some deadly maritime tragedies.

Jules doubted we would be attempting Hell Gate. But what if Neil wanted to risk it to save time? What if foul weather held us up earlier in our voyage and he had to get back fast to go off and fight in another war or something? It's also tempting to take it because it means less time out in the Atlantic Ocean.

Later, Jules and Neil came over to our house with large nautical charts and laid them out on our dining room table so we could study our intended course. Seeing we would be sailing about 10 miles out from the New Jersey Shore to avoid waves and other currents, I realized I wasn't going to be yelling "ahoy there" to anyone crazy enough to be sunbathing on the beach. At 10 miles out, would there be rogue waves to contend with? Pirates? Although Neil was a trained fighter having served in two Middle East wars, I decided to pack my own knife.

What about sudden squalls? Normally I liked that word, but I sure didn't want to be caught in one in the Atlantic Ocean. Jules and Neil assured us that the weather station would be on at all times, and that the Coast Guard could easily be reached by calling 16 on the radio. (Note to self: learn what the radio looks like, where it is, and how to use it.)

As we discussed our course around Manhattan (much to my dismay, Neil said we *would* be sailing through Hell Gate to avoid the Atlantic), Jim noticed we would sail through a place called Gravesend Bay. He said, "I'm sure that name is just an exaggeration, right?" After reading how Hell Gate got its name, I didn't want to know how Gravesend Bay got its.

I did, however, finally work up the nerve to ask Jules what a sailing harness was and why my neighbor suggested I borrow hers. "Actually," she replied, "that's not a bad idea. It's a way to tie yourself onto the boat's lifeline to prevent any erratic waves and wind from knocking you overboard." The truth was finally coming out—there was just a little more risk to this trip than microwaving popcorn! If I accidentally fell overboard, would my first worry be drowning, freezing or shark attack? (Note to self: bring an even bigger knife and keep it in my boot.)

Next, Neil showed us a YouTube video of people sailing a boat similar to theirs. It looked fun to hoist a sail up and down. When I asked what they taught their Special Olympic sailing athletes, Jules replied, "We teach them how to work the jib."

I asked, "Can you at least teach Jim and me how to work the jib?"

Suddenly sounding very Navy, Neil declared, "Oh you'll be doing a lot more than working the jib! We are going to be sailing 18 hours a day, so there will be a lot of work for everyone. We will be drinking hot tea all day and night to keep warm. We must stay alert and ready for anything."

So I had been shanghaied too! Gone were the promises of leisurely dinners at marinas, movies and cheap wine. Would we be swabbing the deck form dawn till dusk? If Jim and I weren't up to snuff, or deemed lazy, would we be flogged? Was keelhauling still legal? How does one stage a mutiny?

What if the sails tore and we ran out of gas—would we be set adrift in the Atlantic? If we were starving, would we resort to cannibalism? When I asked Jules who would be eaten first, she replied, "The least useful."

Thank goodness I was about to make myself useful by taking a four-hour coastal navigation course. It was just going to be a brief overview of a very complicated subject, but at least it was something. Poor Jim, he just didn't have time to become indispensable before the trip.

I kept my family and friends up-to-date on our preparations:

Blog post—Saturday, March 4

Jim and I went to a marine store so he could buy some sailing gloves (ones where his freezing fingers will remain uncovered so he can tie knots) and rubber boots. He actually became excited about our trip when the salesman encouraged him to buy the Greek fisherman's cap he was eyeing.

He told Jim, "You were made for that cap—you look like Zorba the Greek." Though not as practical as the wide-brimmed waterproof hat Jim had tried on earlier, he began fancying himself looking like a rugged seafarer.

His excitement over his purchases dimmed, however, when the salesman also mentioned he should buy a whistle. "Why would I need that?" Jim asked.

The salesman replied, "Didn't you see the movie, *Titanic*?

In the car ride home, I assured Jim that unlike the leading lady in the recent *Titanic* movie, I would share my floatation devise with him so we could *both* whistle for rescue.

That evening, Jim recovered his enthusiasm for the trip when he put on his new, Greek fisherman cap. Clipping off the tag, which showed a bearded sailor smoking a pipe with rolling seas behind him, Jim flipped it over to read the manufacturer's (Aegean) statement: "...one does not need to be Greek, or a fisherman, to wear our caps. However, a feeling for adventure and romance is a must!"

"Hey, that's me!" Jim said. He was finally coming around—just in time for our "set sail" date next week on March 10th. Strolling hand in hand through Mystic that night, we were excited to embark on a new adventure together—one that would make our house worthy to be placed on the Mystic Seafarer's Trail.

Many of our landlubbing New York family and friends were excited for us and enjoyed my updates. But should I share with them some of the very real dangers we would face? Do I tell them that I prepared our daughter Jackie for the worst and told her who to call regarding our assets? That we decided it was too risky to bring Bailey and instructed the kennel who to contact if we never showed up to collect him? Would I cause my family worry if I revealed that our sailing master, Jules, was completely blind? Would they understand, as our seasoned Mystic sailor friends did, that since no sailor can see the wind, why would Jules need to?

When asked how she can sail around without seeing anything, Jules said, "I trim the sails according to the wind. I take most of my clues from the direction of the wind, but I get verbal clues from the crew to indicate danger such as rocks, buoys and lobster pots [basket-like traps]."

Happy when on the water, Jules said she likes to thinks about wind Scriptures such as, "The wind blows where it wishes and you hear the sound of it, but do not know where it comes from and where it is going; so is everyone who is born of the Spirit." (John 3:18)

In the end, I decided to tell everyone everything. Let all share in the terror and thrills as our voyage unfolded.

My mother, an adventuress herself, was excited that I was embarking on a great sea voyage—a once in a lifetime opportunity she said. She loved telling her bridge club all about my preparations. She had always been rather disappointed by my fear of the horse her parents had given me to ride on their farm. Now I had to a chance to prove my bravery.

My father, on the other hand, was worried sick. When last sailing the Long Island Sound as a passenger, he spent time calculating his distance from land, and came to the conclusion that he could survive a two-mile swim to shore if necessary. Given the time of year I would be sailing, however, he knew I would never be able to swim that far without giving into hypothermia first.

Now, do I tell Jules that it's not quite true that I had never sailed before? That when I was a teenager, I went sailing with a friend and her dad and tore their very expensive sail by raising it incorrectly? That I must have "heaved" instead of "hoed?" That after 35 years, I can still see that father's expression as we quietly motored back to the marina? And that Jim was actually a sailing student dropout at a boy's sleep away camp because his instructor kept shouting at him for mishandling the boat—saying his actions were about to overturn it?

I decided that Jules, as Sailing Master, deserved full disclosure. In her role as a social worker, she has worked with the criminally insane. Surely she could handle a couple of incompetent sailors!

Blog post: Monday, March 5

I just completed a four-hour navigational class. I am shocked to learn what lies beneath the waters along the east coast. Sailing charts are full of symbols warning of all kinds of hazards—rocks, underwater ship wrecks, and even unexploded depth charges!

I also learned that the numbers printed throughout the water part of the chart is the depth of the water at low tide—important to know when trying to find a marina that will accommodate the draft (depth of the boat in water) of your vessel.

Well, I gotta go. Jules just called and asked me to come over to practice getting into their "man overboard" harness. She said, "You don't want to fall overboard this time of year, but if you do, it's a lot easier for me to teach you how to get into this harness on my floor than in the cold water!"

Blog post: Thursday, March 8

Jim's been complaining that I'm buying us a lot of gear for what was supposed to be a free vacation. So, when I bought myself a headlamp, something you'd see a miner wear, I didn't get him one.

"Hey," he said, "if you get to have one, then I want one too."

So, I went back to the store. He tried his on yesterday morning while eating breakfast. He finally admitted that it does come in handy. "Now I can really see my cereal!"

Since learning how to spot unexploded depth charges on nautical charts, I thought I should move on to study the survival books I've collected over the years. *The Worst-Case Scenario Survival Handbook* was great for showing me how to jump into a dumpster from a building, but it only had a page on how to fend off a shark attack or treat frost bite. My *US Army Survival Manual* featured mostly how to survive on land—from jungle to desert—but it did have a chapter on sea survival.

Well, I'm off to the bookstore now to find out how to live for months on the open sea without resorting to cannibalism. Jim shouldn't complain about that purchase.

15 SHANGHAIED PART III

I decided it was better for Jim and me to be safe than sorry, so I bought sailing harnesses at a marine consignment store.

While Bailey barked from my car at the store owner's dog, Schooner, I told the woman our winter sailing plans. As she demonstrated how to wear the harness and tether and clip it to the boat's life line, she said, "Wow, you are braver than I am—and I live on a sailboat!"

Was I brave—or just naïve?

Plopping my purchases in the car next to Bailey, I glanced back at Schooner on his leash out front to say goodbye. Suddenly, I caught sight of a sign posted next door at the Law Office of Richard D. Dixon. Dixon was offering this village of seafarers, which now included me, his estate services to "…chart a course for smooth sailing throughout your life's voyage."

When our lawyer son-in-law had learned of our sailing trip, he asked if our wills were in order. And now, only days before we were to embark on our epic voyage, was another estate reminder. Why was I noticing this sign now? Was this sign "a sign?"

My next problem was to figure a way to silence Jim's complaints about my harness purchases. I had told him our new headlamps and foul weather gear would make walking Bailey in the next hurricane a better, safer experience. With the addition of our harnesses, I would stress the advantage of walking Bailey hands-free, now possible because we could loop his leash through the big rings attached to the front of them.

I still had yet to buy bottles of vitamin C and lots of oranges (because I don't like limes) in an effort to stave off scurvy. When I asked Dr. Lee McDowell, author of *Vitamin History, the early years*, when we would begin suffering from scurvy should we get set adrift at sea, he said it could be in as little as six weeks, "though generally it takes 10-12 weeks for scurvy to develop."

Seafarers have suffered from scurvy throughout the ages. In 1749, an onboard experiment showed that oranges and lemons cured scurvy, but it was not until the late 1700s that the British navy required ships to carry citrus juice.

Scurvy, McDowell said, is what led to the deaths of the majority of the *Mayflower* passengers who died that first winter of 1620-1621 (approximately half out of 102 died). Early symptoms of scurvy include bleeding gums, gingivitis, loosening teeth and "breath of a filthy savor." As scurvy progresses, people become too weak to walk. "With scurvy, there is weakening of collagenous structures in bones, cartilage, teeth and connective tissue, swollen bleeding gums, with loss of teeth; fatigue and lethargy, rheumatic pain in legs, degeneration of muscles and skin hemorrhage."

It was the bad breath that worried me—Jules, Neil, Jim and I would be in awfully tight quarters with each other on their boat.

My genetic heritage gave me hope that I would be the last of the group to succumb to scurvy since I descend from surviving Mayflower passenger Richard Warren. He was one of eight married men who made it out of 24 that first winter. Oh brother, that meant I was going to have to take care of everyone else while they slowly wasted away.

Blog post: Friday, March 9

Right now Jim and I are on the Amtrak train heading to Washington, D.C., to see our daughter Jackie. She will take us to Annapolis on Saturday to meet Jules and Neil at a marina on the Chesapeake Bay.

I was stunned when the conductor said we were crossing over Hell Gate Bridge, which is directly over the most treacherous passage of our whole trip. Now I can understand Humphrey Bogart's dread in the movie *African Queen* when he faced the wild, unpredictable currents of the Ulanga River. The currents under Hell Gate Bridge were going in so many directions, I can see how you can get caught in a whirlpool.

Blog post: Saturday, March 11

Tonight is the night we board the sloop *Watercolors* to join Jules and Neil.

We had our last good night's sleep at a Holiday Inn in Arlington, VA. I felt so guilty that Jim and I relaxed last night while Jules and Neil drove down with all our gear, their gear, plus their heavy boat batteries, etc. Upon arriving, they had to spend the entire night de-winterizing the boat and prepare it for immediate sail.

Jules started blogging her version of our trip. She told on me that instead of helping them with last minute preparations before leaving Mystic, I got my hair dyed so I could look good as I wave to all the onlookers on shore.

Blog post: Monday, March 13

For those of you who don't already know what's happened, you can begin uncovering the story by reading an excerpt of our daughter Jackie's e-mail to my parents. She wanted to be the first to fill them in on what had transpired since picking us up from Union Station in Washington, D.C.:

The Lisa and Jim Story: Adventure on the High Seas
As told by their daughter, impartial bystander, Jackie Tortora

On Friday, March 9, 4:30 p.m., I received a text from my mom that she and Dad had arrived in Union Station in D.C. I left my office and walked next door to Union Station where I found Mom with an enormous pack on her back (looking like a European backpacker carrying 30 pounds of stuff) and Dad who was carrying a large duffel bag, looking like he wanted to set it down.

We went to dinner at a nice little Greek restaurant. As my Mom was sipping red wine and generously buttering a large platter of dinner rolls, she voiced concern that Neil and Jules were stuck with all the horrid tasks of readying and de-winterizing the boat while she sat in this heated restaurant eating chicken kabobs and stuffed Portabella mushrooms. "I feel guilty," she said, savoring another sip of wine. Something made me wonder if she really did feel guilty. I think she was very happy to escape the manual labor part of the trip.

Paul [Jackie's husband] and I took Mom and Dad to the quaint, touristy part of Annapolis the following day to wait for Jules and Neil, who would be sailing in to pick them up on their way to a nearby remote marina called Carr Creek. After a tough day of sailing, Jules and Neil finally showed up around 8 p.m. They loaded my parent's train luggage, plus 20 bags full of "worst case scenario" supplies that Mom insisted they buy at Target, on their sail boat. My parents' "room," or more accurately, a bed in a cupboard, was about the size of two small desks. It was already filled to the brim with the massive amount of luggage they gave to Jules and Neil to lug from Mystic. I had no idea how they would fit on their bed. Maybe Mom would make Dad sleep on top of it.

The toilet was inside the shower. Since they weren't going to waste electricity on a luxury like hot water, they wouldn't be showering much on this trip. But if they did, they would simply cover the toilet with wooden slats, which then made it a shower. Paul was very interested in the possibility of showering while using the toilet at the same time. He figured that would save hours of time over the span of his life.

Paul also said going on a boat seemed like a punishment. He said he could just picture his Dad threatening him with it when he was misbehaving as a child. "That's it! You're going on the boat!"

As we waved goodbye to my parents, Paul asked why no one was able to talk my parents out of this. I assured him my dad was not thrilled, but Mom was determined to have her adventures and stories.

The next morning, Sunday, I received a text from my mom saying that Neil and Jules decided to remain at the marina in Annapolis instead of sailing on to the remote, cheaper marina. This made Mom very happy. She was able to have her Starbucks in the morning before they set sail.

Later that day, at about 5 p.m., I received another text from mom. She was terrified and wanted to get off the boat immediately. She asked me and her friend Cindy to Google ways to get her out of there. Hours later, at approximately 2 a.m., the seafarers made it to a marina half way through the Chesapeake & Delaware Canal to Bear, Delaware. After a few hours' sleep, they parted ways.

Upon abandoning ship, Mom and Dad took a half-hour cab ride to Wilmington, DE, and, as I write this, are on a train heading back to Mystic.

I am missing many details, but I'm sure Mom will fill in the gaps later.

Love, Jackie

Tuesday, March 14

My e-mail to friends and family:

Now that I'm safely on shore and had a decent night's sleep, I will try to "fill in the gaps."

Though many understand my reasons for deserting our friends in Delaware, my own mother was disappointed. "You wimp," she said, when I called from the train to tell her the news. Upset that I had abandoned my friends, she added, "Bad girl." I guess she was dreading what to tell her bridge club.

My dad's reaction to my abandoning ship? "Thank God!"

So, how could I abandon our friends after only 36 hours on the boat? Especially since I needed this epic adventure to write my international bestseller?

Prior to the trip, I had imagined that even if Neil and Jim succumbed to some weird, incapacitating illness, Jules and I would brave any hardship together to get our men safely back to Mystic. Our adventure was going to be so "edge-of-your-seat exciting" it would be included in the next edition of Life Book's, *The Greatest Adventures of All Time*. Alongside Amelia Earhart's quest to circumnavigate the globe would be our story, titled something like, "Plump Writer and Blind Sailor Defy Foul Weather, Scurvy, and Temptation to Eat Useless Crew Members."

Perhaps you are wondering if I jumped ship because all my Mystic sailor friends were right—that the cold, erratic winds of March made this an extremely dangerous trip? Or, you already heard some of the obstacles we faced, making you a little sympatric?

Although I *was* alarmed at the sight of water seeping onto our cabin floor the morning of our departure, it turned out to be from an overflowing water tank. Jules and I remedied the situation within an hour by sopping up the water with rags and wringing them out into buckets. No, the fear of a damaged hull was not why I left my friends. Surprisingly enough, it really wasn't any of the day's miseries that made me jump ship—although they certainly didn't help.

The simple fact is—at a very inopportune time—I found out that I am terrified of sailing. I never considered that could happen as I always enjoyed being a passenger on a motorboat, large or small, in a river or in the ocean. But lazing around on a motorboat is a vastly different experience than sailing a small boat in big water.

Shortly after the sails went up that first morning, Jules and Neil's sailboat tipped (heeled) heavily to one side, putting me into an absolute panic. Every time we ticked and tacked, or jibbed and jabbed (the actual sailing maneuvers are called jibe and tack), my panic rose afresh as the boat decided which way to lean, tossing the bags of Target supplies and Vitamin C bottles I neglected to stow (secure) throughout the deck below. Although I brought my sailing harness, I had forgotten to put it on. I was too afraid once we set sail to go below to find it—what if we capsized and I was trapped?

Without my harness, I was unattached to the boat. I constantly imagined myself falling overboard into the very cold water. At this time of year, hypothermia would set in long before I could reach the Maryland shore, which seemed very far away from the middle of the Chesapeake Bay. If Jules and Neil managed to fish me out with their "man overboard device," they would have to strip off all my wet clothes. I didn't want Neil to see me naked!

While Neil was busy at the helm yelling things like "prepare to tack" or "prepare to jibe," sounding as though we were preparing for battle, Jim and Jules were busy pulling on various ropes (called lines), making the sails go this way and that. I, on the other hand, was busy crying and loudly reciting the Lord's prayer in hopes that God would get me out alive—and if not, prepare my soul for death. As much as I wanted to see our daughter Elizabeth again, I didn't want to go down to an icy grave to do it.

I thought of all those Mystic headstones that read "Lost at Sea." Although it's the Mystic way to go, my grave was next to Elizabeth's in a landlubbing part of New York. What would people think if "Lost at Sea" was on my headstone there?

Neil asked Jim to calm me down, but Jim couldn't handle more tasks— he was too busy ticking and tacking. The action never ceased. In my mind, every tack and jibe presented the possibility of the sails tearing, leaving us dead in the water. Unlike Jules's favorite calming Scripture about the wind, the following describes what's really going on at sea: "The wind blows to the south and turns to the north; round and round it goes, ever returning on its course" (Ecclesiastes 1:6).

With Jim busy concentrating on his tack and jibe maneuvers, it fell to Jules to help me understand that the boat was in no danger of capsizing. She said things like, "This boat has a keel that's designed to prevent it from tipping over." Well, I was sure that the *Titanic* had a very nice keel too.

"Lisa," Jules insisted, "sailing is really not *that* dangerous."

Neil laughed, "Jules, don't say things like 'not *that* dangerous.' Come on, you're a therapist, I'm sure you can do better than that."

The laughter got me to relax—a little. I thought of our new sailboat painting hanging over the fireplace. Depicting a schooner racing in the America's Cup, it looked so graceful leaning to one side as it sliced through the sea. Landlubbers have no idea what it's like to be in one of those heeling boats!

Jules finally managed to calm me down enough so I could go below to use the bathroom. Just as I was about to decide sailing was tolerable when given a chance to get used to it, a sudden heave in the boat brought the water so close to the bathroom window I imagined it smashing through. I ran back up on deck as fast as I could.

Moments later, Neil looked concerned. He calmly asked Jim to go below and read some numbers on a board above the navigation table. Jim yelled out, "10.5, 8.5, 7…the numbers keep going down."

I looked at Jules's face to see what they were talking about. Expressionless. No one would look at me. Finally Jules said, "Jim, can you get my cell phone? I need to make a call."

They finally told me what I didn't want to hear. "The boat battery is dead." I knew what a dead battery meant—a dead GPS. And, a dead boat motor also makes maneuvering through channels and marinas very difficult.

I had taken that navigation class for just this purpose, but in my fright, I couldn't remember how to look at a chart and figure out our coordinates. Neil, however, used his dividers and chart and gave our position to the boat service guy Jules reached on her phone (boaters have their own kind of triple A). Knowing that we were still sailing north, the service guy kept calling Jules for updates on our position until he could get there. In the meantime, the boat radio, which relentlessly scanned the air waves, broadcast a distressed caller asking the Coast Guard for rescue. Why on earth did I think sailing would be fun? It's scarier than riding a horse!

No wonder author Herman Melville abandoned ship, preferring to take his chances among cannibals. Anything is safer than sailing!

When the repair man finally arrived in his small motor boat to fix the battery, he appeared happy and carefree. He called out, "Hi Everybody! It's a nice day for sailing isn't it?"

Here was my chance to yell back "Ahoy there!" yet I said nothing. I just stared at his boat trying to figure out how to become a stowaway on it. I just had to get off this sailboat.

No, I couldn't abandon Jim and my friends. I resisted the urge—at the moment. But what if the battery failed again *and* our sails ripped, making it impossible to maneuver the boat at all? What if we were on the Atlantic stretch of our trip when that happened? We could be washed out to sea. It was already apparent to all who the most useless member of our sailing party was—who would be eaten first should the need arise. It was me!

After the boat repair man departed, my only hope now was for Neil to get us to a marina as soon as possible. They were few and far between because many are not open until April or May.

When no one was looking, I texted Jackie and my kayaking friend Cindy asking if they could figure out a way to get me out of there. They came up with various routes back to Mystic depending on which marina we pulled into.

Finally, close to midnight, we made an approach to a dark marina near the entrance to the Chesapeake and Delaware Canal. Feeling confident that land was soon at hand, I lay down below deck to relax on the salon bench (with my winter coat and mittens on of course).

Suddenly, I became aware that everyone topside had stopped talking, making it eerily quiet. Going on deck to find out why, I noticed in horror that the instrument measuring water depth was showing a reading too low for our sloop. Neil had previously phoned the marina asking if they were in a spot deep enough to accommodate his 4.7 foot draft, and they said yes. Either they had misinformed him, or the sandy bottom had shifted in the current.

Although his quick maneuvering got us off the bottom, I knew for certain that a sailor's life was not for me. Moment later, when we were almost run over by a city-block size tanker trying to squeeze past us in the dark, narrow Chesapeake and Delaware Canal, I was convinced of it.

We pressed deeper into the canal looking for the next open marina. Although Neil had checked ahead to make sure the sloop's 51 foot main mast would clear the bridges and low-lying power lines that stretched across the canal, I still held my breath as we approached each one (I ran below deck when we closed in on the power lines thinking I'd be less electrocuted there).

In between moments of terror that night, I tried searching for that all-important North Star. I just had to prove my worth as a navigator should we get swept out to sea, but I couldn't find it. (To find it, you must locate the lower two-star cup part of the Big Dipper, then look off to the right until you find the end of the Little Dipper.)

There was no doubt about it. I was the most useless crew member on this trip. I knew that my terror would only worsen as the trip progressed into the Atlantic.

Now was the time for me to make a decision. Jules and Neil had a boat to move to Mystic—I didn't want my need to be docked at a marina the whole time to slow them down. So, feeling terribly guilty, upon finally docking at a marina in the Chesapeake and Delaware Canal at 2 a.m., I informed everyone that I was just too scared to go on. If we were going to jump ship, this was the moment to do it. Jackie and Cindy had texted me various escape options, including the distance to the nearest Amtrak train station, along with a phone number for a cab.

I offered to call some of our friends who wanted to sail as our replacements should something like this happen, but Jules and Neil felt it would be easier to finish the trip themselves. No need for us to plot a mutiny—they were willing to let us go.

All along I thought it would be Jim who would insist we get off so we could enjoy a real vacation with a toothbrush holder. Although he wanted to accompany me home, he had been willing to endure the rest of the trip if I was. He had shown himself a sailor, not a coward.

Before parting ways, Jules, ever the therapist, began strategizing how to help me overcome my fear of sailing upon their return to Mystic. She and Neil would take me out again on a calm, warm day in local waters, so I could see the familiar coastline. Jules said, "I don't want you to panic every time you see a triangular piece of cloth!" With so many triangle-shaped pieces of cloth moving through Mystic, she was right. I did need to get cured of my sail phobia—fast!

Having witnessed first-hand the fearless sailing techniques of Jules who, though blind, went topside to fiddle around with the sails despite the possibility of being tossed overboard, and Neil as he jibbed and tacked in addition to steering and reading nautical charts, all the while trying to comfort an hysterical friend, has cemented their rightful spot on the Mystic Seafarer's Trail. In my mind, their sailing exploits were just as daring as Amelia Earhart's flying feats.

I, however, will never be counted among the fearless sea voyagers of Mystic. My house will never be deemed worthy to be placed on the Mystic Seafarer's Trail.

Well, thanks for coming along on my almost epic adventure. I hope you're not too disappointed that I was unable to give you a journey worthy of living vicariously through!

Sincerely,

Landlubber Lisa

###

Jules and Neil said I could save face by sneaking aboard their boat when they approached Mystic, but I'd have to remember to look dirty and disheveled before greeting our friends. Too late, I had already e-mailed everyone from the train.

One sailor friend, Nancy, e-mailed me back: "And to think you were disappointed that you'd always be in sight of land. It's okay, Lisa, landlubbers are people, too!"

Kate, the sailing acupuncturist, offered to stick me with some needles to help me de-stress.

Elizabeth, a fearless kayaking buddy of Cindy's, said, "Lisa, face it. You think you want adventure, but what you really want is for others to take the risks so you can live vicariously through them."

Gary, kayaking Cindy's husband, said I would be forever known in Mystic as the "Chicken of the Sea."

One woman, who shall remain nameless because she earns her living teaching others about the sea, thought I deserved some compassion. Pulling me aside, she whispered, "Don't feel bad. I never took to sailing either—despite all the sailing lessons I took."

Friends from New York, however, had an entirely different reaction. Patt and Larry, who had been worrying we preferred the excitement of Jules and Neil to the memory of the many quiet dinners served in their home, were delighted that I had failed as a sailor. Patt e-mailed me: "I just want to let you know that Larry and I are here for you and would never make you toe the line, or hoist the sails. Heck, I wouldn't even let you help me clear the table after a long and filling meal. So when are you moving back to New York?"

Less than two weeks after abandoning ship, I decided I must overcome my fear of sailing as soon as possible. So, I took my first sailing lesson. Never again.

I was forced to sit all alone in a little sailboat and tack and jibe by making figure eights around buoys. Trying to coordinate my movements with the wind reminded me why I begged Jim to drop out of the dancing lessons we took years earlier. I just can't seem to move when and where wind (or music) dictates.

Every time the sailboat was actually being moved along by the wind, I became afraid and released the sail so I could stop (called going into irons)—I just don't like being pushed by a force outside myself. Although it was almost fun to go up the Mystic River in one straight line, to get back, I had to tack and jibe the whole way. Running aground twice, I needed the instructor to tow me back to deeper water. After the second time, I asked him to tow me back to land once and for all.

Happy to end my sailing lesson early, I hopped back into my red convertible, took command of my gas pedal and steering wheel, and was on my way. Always obedient, my car does exactly what I tell it to do, when I tell it to do it.

A few days later, I visited the open, three-sided seaside chapel on Enders Island, the place where the worried and broken-hearted leave their hand-written prayers. Some of the words are so personal and moving, I feel like I'm standing on Holy Ground.

One particular prayer caught my attention—one I should have placed there myself before my failed epic sea voyage. On a tiny scrap of paper held down by a rock was a note that read, "Oh Lord, your sea is so great and my boat is so small. Help me." There were two initials and the date: March 17, 2012. I don't know if the writer was referring to life in general, or if he/she was actually going on a long sea voyage in a tiny craft. I guess I'll never know.

When I told my Bible study group about the boat prayer I found in the seaside chapel, some questioned if I was "allowed" to read those private words. I told everyone I thought that if a prayer was only folded in half, it was fair game—and I would add my prayer to the writer's. If a prayer was tightly folded up, then I wouldn't open it. Most agreed that sounded O.K. (My Bible group hinted they might be willing to buy this book if they saw their names mentioned. Those who worried about prayer privacy were Jeff, Shannon, Christine, Mike and Denise.)

In an attempt to create a new life for myself apart from sailing, I phoned kayaker Cindy and begged her to take me kayaking again. I promised I would no longer paddle alongside her making comments such as, "I wish I could find a friend with a sailboat."

So, like Dorothy of *The Wizard of Oz,* who clicked her ruby slippers together and said, "There's no place like home," I zipped up my life vest, plopped down into Cindy's kayak, and thought, "There's no boat like a kayak."

As we paddled together in Stonington Harbor, I realized we were much closer to the Atlantic than when we kayaked in Mystic. I suddenly recalled a TV show where two kayakers were swept out to sea. The stronger paddler managed to reach shore, leaving the weaker one to fend for himself. (Note to self: be nice to Cindy.)

Being in Stonington Harbor, I finally had my chance to get a closer look at the partially submerged schooner *Marmion.* With its masts still exposed, I was able to see its rigging and mossy deck. According to her former captain, Katie Bradford, owner of Custom Marine Canvas, the *Marmion* "was built in 1927 in Coconut Grove, Florida. Purposely built for pleasure cruises in the shallow waters of the Bahamas, she had a bronze 'shoe,' a thick layer at the front of the keel to crush the coral heads. Later in her career, *Marmion* was converted from a ketch to a schooner."

No, Katie didn't run aground with the *Marmion.* Katie said, 'She sank due to the neglect of her mahogany deck. The mahogany needed to be kept constantly wet to keep the boards from shrinking and letting water in."

Katie's first mate on *Marmion* was teenager Andrea Lee of Mystic. In the summer of 1984, while Katie was participating in an event called Tall Ships Boston with *Marmion*, Andrea was racing the tall ship *Marques* from Bermuda to Nova Scotia. On June 3, the *Marques* encountered a sudden squall shortly after 4 a.m. that knocked her over. It sank in less than a minute. Half of the *Marques*'s 28-person crew were between the ages of 15 and 25 and many were asleep below deck when the squall hit. Andrea, at age 19, was one of 19 who perished aboard the ship.

Katie happened to meet one of the nine survivors, Robert (Bobby) Cooper of Belfast, Ireland, in St. Thomas when she sailed the *Marmion* there for the winter. When she asked Robert to tell her about the tragedy, he told her that Andrea shooed him through the companionway ahead of him.

As far as I know, only one body was recovered.

Unable to get the account of Andrea Lee out of my mind, I visited the Mystic Seaport Collections Resource Center to read eye witness accounts of the tragedy from the survivors. According to an article in *Soundings* (Aug. 1984), 16-year-old Clifton McMillan of Fairfield, Conn., was in the galley when the squall hit. He was quoted as saying, *"The water started pouring in…about five of us below struggled to get out, but only three of us made it, I think. I noticed a raft in front of me and jumped on to it as the boat started to sink."*

An article in *Motor Boating & Sailing* (Aug. 1984) added to the image of the horror with its headline, *"Tall Ship Tragedy: The four-paned windows in the poop cabin, where Captain Finlay must have been struggling to get out with his wife and toddler son, were the last of the* Marques *seen by those thrown overboard…"*

It's too hard for me to write much more about this at the moment. Now that I've been sailing and know many sailors, the tragedy feels too close to home. Andrea Lee was one of two Mystic Seaport staff members who perished in sinking. Five days after the tragedy, her family scheduled a memorial service for her on the whaleship *Charles W. Morgan* on June 8th at 6 p.m.

I dedicated this book to those who have been lost at sea because I feel like I got to know some of those who never made it back to Mystic to receive a "proper" burial. Knowing how hard it was to leave our daughter's grave behind in New York, I can't imagine having no grave at all to visit. After climbing over another stone wall to get into an Old Mystic graveyard, I found this inscription on the headstone of a ship captain who died at sea:

> *The dust may sleep 'neath sea or sod;*
> *From each the soul mounts up to God;*
> *Not watery tomb, nor marble walls,*
> *Can hold the spirit when He calls.* lxxix

I hoped those lines comforted his family—and others who mourn "lost at sea" loved ones.

Although I have decided that kayaking in Mystic is about as adventurous as I care to be at the moment, I haven't completely given up on the idea of embarking on another sea voyage—but this time, in a little more comfort.

When Cindy took me down the Mystic River on my most recent trip, and we paddled past several luxurious, motorized yachts, I couldn't help but think, "Wow, if I could only find a friend with one of those!"

EPILOGUE

I've come to the conclusion I'm too scared of ending up like Amelia Earhart to accomplish any of the daring deeds she did. Although I have resigned myself to remain the lady who only reads or writes about the brave exploits of others, instead of having them herself, I will not give in to despair. I may never be asked by Mystic Seaport to be a speaker for their "Adventure Series" talks, but I have returned to sailing with Jules and Neil. I even bring Bailey along—and he loves it!

At the present, Jules and Neil only take us as far as Noank or Stonington, and if there is a stiff wind, they don't take full advantage of it in order to keep the boat more upright and to my liking.

Jules and Neil also fulfilled a secret fantasy of mine. They sailed Jim and me to Skipper's Dock, the restaurant in Stonington seen in the movies *Mystic Pizza* and *Hope Springs*. I have always wanted to sail up to that restaurant and sit down to eat. When we arrived, Jules threw the line to a man waiting to tie us up, and we disembarked, along with Jules's guide dog, to eat dinner on the deck. I wanted to wear my life preserver while we ate so everyone would know I'd just come off the water, but Jules wouldn't let me.

Although my failed epic sea voyage means my home doesn't deserve to be on the Mystic Seafarer's Trail, there is still hope it may get on anyway. Why? Because on Sunday, September 9, 2012, Jim and I held an impromptu wedding reception for Jules and Neil in our backyard.

Someday, the world may be as interested to know where they had their wedding as they are in where Amelia had hers. And just like Amelia, they barely gave anyone notice. Jules couldn't stand thinking about wedding preparations anymore, so she called me one evening to say she and Neil were just going to do it—now (and no, she wasn't pregnant).

In preparation for this quick, but shotgun-less wedding, Jules and Neil let me come with them to Groton Town Hall so I could watch them apply for their marriage license—this was about as close as I was ever going to get to following in Amelia Earhart's footsteps.

Before signing their application form, Jules and Neil were asked by the clerk to raise their right hands and swear that everything on the form was accurate and true. Were Earhart and Putman required to do that? If so, did Amelia cringe inside recalling her lie about her age?

I begged Jules and Neil to let us hold a small wedding reception at our home. I just had to play a part in this historic moment—had to get my house on the Mystic Seafarer's Trail somehow. They agreed.

The morning of the wedding, our daughter Jackie consulted with me by text about the flower and table arrangements. Jackie had worried that since Cindy and I were in our 50s, and Jules in her 30s, we might try to take advantage of Jules's blindness by decorating the house in some out-of-date style. I sent Jackie photos of our table arrangement through our phones so she could see what Cindy and I were going for. She approved of the centerpiece once we surrounded it with color-coordinated antique books.

Before coming to our house, where Kayak Cindy became Caterer Cindy, Jules and Neil got married at the Chapel on the Thames at the Naval Submarine Base. Prior to the ceremony, Jim joined Neil on base and watched him carefully place all his service medals, including those received during times of war, on his white uniform. At the non-denominational chapel, which housed a statue of Mary holding a submarine, Kate, the sailing acupuncturist, played Irish wedding music on her concertina (a type of accordion). My job was to remind Jim to grab Neil's cap (Neil calls it a "cover") off the bench and hand it to him before he left the church after the ceremony. Our reptile-loving friend Fran served as wedding cake picker-upper and photographer. Just as in Amelia Earhart's wedding where George Putnam slipped a platinum ring on Amelia's finger, Neil slipped a platinum ring on Jules's finger (don't worry, Neil got one too). And, just like Amelia, Jules kept her maiden name because she was already known professionally by it.

Once back at our house, we gave the bride and groom a Champagne toast on our patio and reminisced how it had only been a year since the Hurricane Irene rotting meat parties brought us closer together.

Anne, a sailing friend of Jules and Neil, was at the reception (the three of them were sailing with the Special Olympics the morning of the wedding). It was at Anne's suggestion we got Jim's shaving cream and wrote "Just Married—Finally!" and tied tin cans to Neil's car. Not having thought about the cans ahead of time, Anne and Jim scrounged around in our recycle bins in the garage until they found a can from the olives Cindy opened for the reception. Kate had the unpleasant job of crawling under the car on our gravel driveway in her dress to attach the can. Although it was only one can, it made enough racket to serve its purpose as they drove away down Allyn Street.

Anne is always one for ideas—some much more glamorous than foraging through recycle bins. At a dinner party given a few weeks before the wedding, she turned to me in all seriousness and said, "I was offered a job sailing someone's yacht to Bermuda. Do you want to help me get it there?"

The whole table erupted in laughter at the very idea of me sailing away from the shores of Mystic—especially into the Bermuda triangle! I guess

Cindy's Gary is right—I'll be forever known as "Chicken of the Sea."

When Jules and Neil become famous for their seafaring voyages, I will mark my house with a plaque stating: "JULES AND NEIL HAD THEIR WEDDING RECEPTION HERE." And someday, a writer will find this short account of their wedding in a little folder at the Mystic River Historical Society. That story hunter will be just as excited as I was when I discovered the Noank Historical Society's file on Amelia Earhart.

Recently, a new friend gave me a small taste of what it would be like to be a celebrity. At a barbeque hosted by Jules and Neil at their marina, Cindy (not the kayaking one, but the one who took my photo for the back cover), asked Neil for a tour of his and Jules's sailboat. She said, "I want to see where Lisa slept in the V-berth and where she went to the bathroom. I especially want to see where she stood crying and texting her daughter looking for ways off."

Also at this barbeque were newcomers, Zack and Lisa. Transferred here by the Coast Guard, Zack told us of his first sail in the Long Island Sound on the Coast Guard's sail-training vessel *Eagle*, a large, three-masted ship taken from the Germans after World War II. On one particularly windy day on the Sound, Zach experienced 13-15 foot seas and a lot of boat heeling.

Zack and Lisa, in turn, were interested to hear my opinion of heeling boats and all about our near-epic sea adventure. This time, Jim didn't interrupt my story-telling by saying the seas weren't really that rough and the boat didn't really heel that close to the water, etc. There was no way he wanted risk another sea voyage just so I could have a more dramatic tale to tell.

The stories in Mystic never end. Where seafarers gather, there is always a voyage to recount or one to plan. Although my cousin Captain Sisson's grave marker declares that his "voyage is ended," for those of us still in the land of the living, it may be just beginning!

THE END

P.S. When I gave a talk to a local group on my sailing misadventure, I provided a PowerPoint presentation so the audience could see what I looked like on the boat—before and after crying to get off. When I recounted the rolling seas and the boat heeling so far over it nearly lay sideways on the water, the only photo I have of that part of my story ruins the dramatic impact. It shows me wearing an unstylish orange life preserver and nerdy-looking hat. I appear utterly miserable while clutching the boat—which is barely heeling at all. The seas behind me appear calm and sparkling. (Note to self: never show that image again—it's a real story squasher.)

I have not given up hope for another epic adventure. Finding a shipwreck is my next goal—without becoming involved in one myself. Jim just bought me the book the beer-making shipwreck discoverer recommended, and I'm reading it now. I also looked at the collection of shipwreck books held in the Mystic Seaport Collections Resource Center—there are so many! Now that Jules and Neil's boat is outfitted with sonar, I think it's possible we could find a shipwreck.

In the meantime, I will continue my quest to get the media to listen to me in regard to how a woman can take steps to prevent congenital CMV from happening to her child. I hope to make that prevention message just as well-known as the "don't change kitty litter" warning for pregnant women. I recently went to San Francisco, where Captain Sisson supposedly failed to find gold, to speak at the international Congenital CMV Conference. I also listened to doctors give the results of their latest findings, CMV prevention and treatment methods, and progress on a vaccine. A vaccine that would prevent congenital CMV, and the kind of disabilities our daughter faced, is all the gold I really need.

THE END—FINALLY!

Lisa and Jules sailing with their dogs.

PREQUEL: MY LIFE BEFORE MYSTIC

Jim and I first visited Mystic in 2006 to get away from our home in Suffern, New York, a few months after Elizabeth died. Mystic seemed shrouded in mystery as a spring fog settled over the river, its tall ships and streets lined with historic homes. The quaint, seafaring community was a welcome break from our grief and humdrum lives as inlanders.

Intrigued by the 19th century maritime village portrayed at Mystic Seaport, we bought blue water glasses from its gift shop etched with the *Charles W. Morgan*, the oldest wooden whaleship in the world. In a park-like cemetery, we took numerous photos of granite headstones engraved with anchors and ships.

Imagining the exciting lives of Mystic's residents, living and dead, set my imagination on fire. Returning home to upstate New York, we hung those photos on our bedroom wall as a reminder of another world—one I wished to escape to.

To make a long story short (aren't you relieved when writers state that?), four years later, my husband's company offered to transfer him to Groton, Connecticut. When I got the news, there was no doubt that I wanted to go and where I wanted to live—right in Mystic.

My life prior to moving to Mystic is told in my memoirs, *Anything But A Dog!* and *Ride a Horse, Not an Elevator*. Although *Ride a Horse* is called a children's novel, it's basically true—except where I conquer my fear of horses (I still can't seem to conquer it) to ride off alone to get help for my grandfather after he is injured by a charging cow.

ABOUT THE AUTHOR

Lisa Saunders is an award-winning writer and speaker living in Mystic, Connecticut, with her husband and hound. She works as a part-time history interpreter at Mystic Seaport and is a member of the Mystic River Historical Society and Daughters of the American Revolution. A graduate of Cornell University, she is the author of several books and a winner of the National Council for Marketing & Public Relations Gold Medallion. She is the Congenital CMV Foundation parent representative.

Lisa's other work, plus her free "How To" e-books and availability for speaking, can be found on her website at: www.authorlisasaunders.com. Lisa can be reached directly at saundersbooks@aol.com

EVER TRUE:
A UNION PRIVATE AND HIS WIFE

Reviews:

"The story of how the marriage between Charles and Nancy survives separation, disease, the threat of death, and malicious gossip is compelling."
Pamela Goddard, Ithaca Times

"I was thoroughly fascinated by the letters and much impressed by the artful way the material was woven together. The story is cohesive and informative, but charming and romantic in a very personal way."
Corinne Will, Managing Editor, Heritage Books, Inc.

Excerpt from introduction: I carefully unfolded the stiff yellowed paper, incredulous that I was actually touching a letter written during the American Civil War. It was one of 150 letters written between my great-great grandparents that I had discovered in a small wooden box in my mother's attic in Suffern, New York. The note I held in my hand, authored by Private Charles McDowell to his wife Nancy, was written on a small, plain piece of stationery--not at all fancy like some of the others in the batch which bore sketches of the White House and battle engagements. I gently smoothed it flat on the table, afraid I would tear it. The handwriting was strange, the ink somewhat faded, making it difficult to read. And then suddenly I came upon a word I recognized in an instant--Abe! It read, "We have [Secretary of State] Seward down here about every other day, and sometimes he fetches Old Abe with him and [he] looks about like any old farmer."

In addition to the letters was Nancy's obituary, which reads: "MRS. MCDOWELL IS DEAD - SHOOK HANDS WITH LINCOLN. With the death of Mrs. Nancy Wager McDowell...the town of Sodus probably loses the distinction of having a resident who could boast of having shaken hands and talked with the martyred Lincoln... Mr. McDowell was a member of the Ninth New York Heavy Artillery in the Union Army and it was while stationed near Washington that his wife had an opportunity to speak with the President. Mrs. McDowell passed nearly a year in that vicinity and many were the pies she baked for the soldiers stationed at the capital. Typhoid Fever caused her to return to Alton to the home of her parents..." ("The Record," Sodus, Wayne County, N.Y. September 18, 1931)

I took the collection of letters back to my home in Maryland and began what was to become an exciting ten-year adventure. First I arranged the letters from Charles by date and began to read. Once I grew accustomed to his old-style handwriting and run-on sentences, I felt myself leaving the present and entering his past. I traveled back over 130 years and joined Charles in heart and mind. I felt his loneliness, his boredom, his fear. I laughed when he found a reason to laugh. He and his brother had enlisted despite his Canadian father's pleas to stay out of the war. As the months of his service turned into years, I hurt over his deep longing for his wife and home and for the life and family he left behind in Canada.

In other letters I was shocked to read of the desertions, hangings, amputations, prostitution, and even theft and murder among Union troops. Charles wrote home about the battles of Cold Harbor, Jerusalem Plank Road, Monocacy, Opequon (Winchester), Cedar Creek, the Siege of Petersburg, an attack by Mosby's Men, and the Shenandoah Valley Campaign.

Next I tackled Nancy's writing. As her collection of letters drew to an end, I was completely immersed in her anxious thoughts about Charles's welfare. She hoped there hadn't been a "ball made to kill" him. She hoped he wouldn't get too close to the Southern women when he occupied their homes. She longed for him to return to her--even if it was just for a short furlough. She wrote that she would rather be dead than continue to live the way they were. I now pondered the final years of her life spent rocking in her chair looking out the window. Perhaps she was awaiting her death so Charles could come for her once more...

Published by Heritage Books: 1-800-876-6103, heritagebooks.com. Contact Lisa directly if you would like her to make a presentation.

SHAYS' REBELLION: THE HANGING OF CO-LEADER, CAPTAIN HENRY GALE

Lisa's ancestor, a Revolutionary War veteran, is found guilty of treason and sentenced to be hanged for his leadership role in Shays' Rebellion. More info: www.authorlisasaunders.com

ANYTHING BUT A DOG!
The perfect pet for a girl with congenital CMV
(cytomegalovirus)

The true story of a big, homeless canine and the little girl who needed him.

Reviews:
"Saunders takes readers on a road trip as harrowing as any Dog Whisperer training challenge...Beyond the laughs about a dizzying pet search, Saunders' dog tale is about a mother who candidly reveals her family's burden, love, and acceptance of a daughter born with severe disabilities—and the people, and pets, forever touched by her life."
Tonia Shakespeare, Rockland Magazine

"Sheds light on a disorder that is preventable and not talked about enough. If you're an animal lover, you'll love the critter tales as much as the special-needs storyline...really lifted my spirits." Terri Mauro, About.com

Excerpt from Chapter One:
"Mom, can I have a dog?" my six-year-old daughter Jackie asked, standing next to me while I washed the breakfast dishes.

I cringed. The dreaded day was here—all kids inevitably ask for one. And why wouldn't they? Movie dogs like Lassie drag you from burning buildings and keep you warm when you're lost in a blizzard. But by the time we're adults, we've learned the truth about them: they urinate on your new wall-to-wall carpets, dig holes in your leather recliners to hide their rawhide bones, and bite your neighbor's kid.

"No, you can't have a dog," I said, bracing myself for the age-old argument.

"Why not?" she demanded.

My mind raced for good excuses. Might as well start with the standard one: "A dog is too much work. And I know I'll end up being the one who walks it in the pouring rain."

"I promise I'll take care of it. I will, I really will!" Jackie exclaimed.

"Sure," I thought, "that's what they all say." Avoiding her pleading eyes, I picked up a plate sticky with leftover syrup. "The truth is," I said, "we just can't risk a dog around your sister." I hated admitting that. I didn't want her to blame her little sister, three years younger, for being so fragile. But taking care of Elizabeth, who was quadriplegic from cerebral palsy, was already enough work without adding a dog that might playfully nip at her.

I know! I'll give Jackie the "lip-severing story." That'll convince her we can't have a dog around her sister.

"When I was 13," I began, "I talked Grandma and Grandpa into letting me have a Weimaraner. His name was Bogie—short for Humphrey Bogart—and he was a nipper. One day, my two-year-old cousin Suzannah was playing on the floor underneath the table with a Popsicle stick in her mouth. Bogie snapped at the stick and bit her lip off! My grandmother got the lip off the carpet and wrapped it in a paper napkin to take to the hospital. But it couldn't be sewn back on. A surgeon fixed Suzannah's face, but when we got home, my mother loaded Bogie into the back seat of the car and took him to the vet's. I never saw him again. He took the 'long walk' as they say in the Lady and the Tramp movie."

I paused so Jackie could let the horror of the incident sink in.

But all she wanted to know was, "Where's Suzannah's lip now?"

"Gosh, I don't know! The last time I saw her lip it was stuck to the napkin, all shriveled and mummy-like on my grandmother's bookshelf. But that's beside the point; can't you see how dangerous a dog could be for your sister? She can't speak—how would she call out to us if she was in another room and the dog was bothering her?"...

Originally published in "Anything But a Dog!" (Unlimited Publishing LLC, 2008), used by permission. Please visit http://www.unlimitedpublishing.com/saunders for more information.

SURVIVING LOSS: THE WOODCUTTER'S TALE

The Woodcutter's Tale is a tender fairytale for all ages about the process of healing after the death of a child. The afterword, written by Julie Russell, LCSW, seeks to help individuals understand the grieving process and to return to a life with purpose and meaning. This booklet includes Lisa Saunders' story of how she's trying to move forward in a way that will honor the memory of her child. More info: www.authorlisasaunders.com

RIDE A HORSE, NOT AN ELEVATOR

Lisa leaves the bullies and elevators of New York City to confront the outhouses, horses and eccentric relatives on her grandparents' farm. Chosen by Cornell University for its "Horse Book in a Bucket" program.

Ride a Horse, Not an Elevator, is a children's novel about a test of young courage. In this story, based on the author's childhood summers, Lisa is a chubby city girl searching for friendship and excitement. She leaves home, and the elevators and bullies of a big apartment complex, to spend a summer in the country at her grandparents' farm. Culture shock! Accompanied only by her loyal beagle, Donald Dog, Lisa faces a summer in a very different environment with its own challenges and dangers. Using an outhouse is the least of her problems. She is terrified of her new pony. Lisa's grandfather is injured by a charging cow and needs her to ride the pony to get help. Remembering Grandma's lesson about how love overcomes fear, she pushes herself past her anxieties to ride alone and obtain the help he needs. The book includes recipes from grandma's kitchen.

"A 'warm fuzzy' in paperback form. It is a tangible tale for storytelling that provides a springboard for discussion between children and adults." Ruth Zwick, Educational Director, Sentinel Publications

For more information on *Ride a Horse, Not an Elevator,* or to have Lisa present her book, writer's workshop for children, or the "Horse Book in a Bucket" program, contact her directly at saundersbooks@aol.com or visit: www.authorlisasaunders.com

LISA'S FREE E-BOOKS

Visit Lisa's website at: www.authorlisasaunders.com to download her following free e-books:

How to Get Published

How to Get a Job

How to Promote Your Business (or yourself)

Surviving Loss: The Woodcutter's Tale (also available as a softcover booklet)

LISA'S SPEAKING TOPICS INCLUDE:

1. Graveyard Adventures—you never know who you will meet!
2. The Hanging of Henry Gale—from patriot to traitor in Shays' Rebellion
3. The Seven Wonders of Mystic
4. Finding Humor on Life's Adventures—and Misadventures!
5. Civil War: Union Private & His Wife (available as a talk, one-act play, or combination)
6. How to Get Published
7. How to Get a Job (Lisa is a former employment recruiter)
8. Stop CMV (Lisa is the Congenital CMV Foundation parent representative)
9. How to Get Free Publicity
10. Children's Writing Workshop (Cornell University included *Ride a Horse, Not an Elevator* in its "Horse Book in a Bucket" program)
11. A Time to Weep, A Time to Laugh—Moving forward after the death of a child

Lisa's appearances: USA 9 News… Cornell University… West Point Museum…Washington Independent Writers Association… Centers for Disease Control and Prevention (CDC)… Seward House… Lincoln Depot Museum…Johns Hopkins University… Siemens Healthcare Diagnostics… Rockland and Three Rivers Community Colleges… Daughters of the American Revolution… Civil War Round Tables… Fitch Middle School… Women's Clubs…Genealogical conferences…grammar schools… libraries…Connecticut Authors and Publishers Association.

ADDENDUM #1: CAPTAIN CHARLES C. SISSON TIMELINE & GENEALOGICAL CHART

- July 23, 1826: Charles born in Groton, CT. (Same year as gold-seeking friend Ransford Ashby.)
- 1831: Thomas E. Wolfe born (Civil War sea captain, ship burned, escaped prison).
- Mar. 20, 1831: Ann Sawyer born.
- April 30, 1833: Frances Sawyer born.
- 1850 Census: Charles Sisson lived beside neighbors, little girls Ann and Frances.
- 1850-1851: Sisson, Wolfe and Ashby went to California in search of gold.
- Feb. 12, 1851: Ransford Ashby died at the age of 25 years, 21 days.
- 1851: Sisson goes to sea and is first officer of ship *Marmion* of New York.
- Aug. 24, 1851: Charles married Ann E. Sawyer, daughter of William Sawyer and Lucretia.
- 1852: ship *Wild Pigeon* built for Sisson (he was commander) and others.
- 1854: Launching of *Elizabeth F. Willets*, Sisson part owner.
- Jan. 13, 1855: Sisson leaves New York for San Francisco on the *Elizabeth F. Willets*. (It took him much longer than other ships that left at approximately the same time for San Francisco. Sisson ran into a calm belt off the coast of California, which left him taking 15 days to cover the last 800 miles. He writes: "May 10—3P.M. Anchored S.F. 118 days and 3 hours from New York, and found that I was the Black Sheep out of the fleet. *The Neptune's Car* 102 days, the *Westward Ho* 102 days and the bark *Greenfield* 110 days."
- May 16, 1855: Agnes Freeman Sisson, Charles and Ann's first child, was born May 16, 1855. She died Mar. 19, 1914.
- 1857: Sisson commander of *Mary E. Sutton*. Captain Sisson's name appears on the grave marker of 15-year-old in Wightman burying ground at Center Groton, Connecticut: John Lamphere, born May 2, 1842, Lost in the Pacific Ocean from Ship *Mary E. Sutton*, Capt. Sisson, June 20, 1857.
- Nov. 18, 1857: daughter Ida Sisson was born. She died Sept. 15, 1858. (She was the second out of five daughters.)
- 1858: Charles buys house on West Mystic Ave. (Formerly known as Skippers Lane.)
- 1860: Census—Ann's father William Sawyer is living with Charles and Ann in Groton, CT, household 578/717.

- 1860: Sisson captain of *Aspasia*.
- 1861: Daughter Anna Sisson was born Dec. 12. She died Feb. 22, 1886.
- 1865: Daughter Sarah Sisson was born Sept. 5. She died Mar. 12, 1920.
- 1867: Daughter Ida Sisson was born May 6. She died Jan. 20,1888. Ida married Rossie Brown on May 14, 1887.
- 1871: The son of Thomas Wolfe, Charles Herbert Wolfe, is the 14-year-old ship's boy on the *Bridgewater* under Sisson's command.
- 1871 (April): As commander of *Bridgewater*, Sisson came upon the foundering Swedish bark *Belladonna* and rescued the captain, two mates and 48 seamen at the scene.
- 1875 - 1877: Charles Sisson is Captain of the ship, *Jeremiah Thompson*.
- Nov. 9, 1875: Capt. Thomas E. Wolfe died at the age of 44 years 10 months: "Lost his life while discharging his duty as pilot on board the ill-fated steamship City of Waco at the time of her burning Nov. 9, 1875, off the port of Galveston, Texas.
- May 12, 1876: Ann dies at sea. Her stone states: Ann E. Sawyer...She died 12 May 1876 at sea on ship "Jeremiah Thompson." In Lat. 12 degrees 00' North, Long. 39 degrees 30' West.
- 1877: *Jeremiah Thompson* is hit by a tidal wave while Charles Herbert Wolfe was serving as third mate on it while anchored off Peru, South America (Marshall, 1922)
- 1878: Sisson is commander of *Thomas Dana*.
- Mar. 9, 1878: Charles Sisson and Mrs. Frances Sawyer Wolfe marry.
- 1880: Charles and Frances are in the 1880 census in New London, Groton, CT, district 103, household 230/258 with Charles's children, Frances' children by her first marriage, and Charles's father-in-law.
- Feb. 27, 1885: Charles dies at the age of 58.
- Sept. 4, 1916: Frances J. Sawyer, wife of Wolfe then Sisson, died. She is buried next to Wolfe (age 83).
- April 17, 2011(Sunday): Author Lisa Saunders meets living cousin, Captain Matthew Sisson, while visiting the grave of Captain Charles Sisson. Matthew Sisson and Lisa Saunders descend from Richard and Mary Sisson, an immigrant couple who were in Rhode Island by 1650. Lisa descends from oldest son George, and Matthew Sisson descends from their son James.
- June 23, 2011: Lisa attends Captain Matthew Sisson's Change of Command Ceremony in New London, CT, and meets several more Sisson cousins.
- June 23, 2012: exactly a year after meeting new cousins at the Sisson Change of Command ceremony, Lisa attends Sisson Conference in Albany, New York, to tell the story—and meets a lot more Sisson cousins!

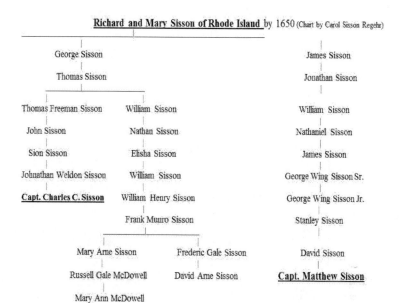

Richard and Mary Sisson of Rhode Island by 1650 (Chart by Carol Sisson Regehr)

George Sisson
|
Thomas Sisson

Thomas Freeman Sisson   William Sisson
|
John Sisson   Nathan Sisson
|
Sion Sisson   Elisha Sisson
|
Johnathan Weldon Sisson   William Sisson
|
Capt. Charles C. Sisson   William Henry Sisson
|
Frank Munro Sisson

Mary Arne Sisson   Frederic Gale Sisson
|
Russell Gale McDowell   David Arne Sisson
|
Mary Ann McDowell
|
Lisa Saunders

James Sisson
|
Jonathan Sisson

William Sisson
|
Nathaniel Sisson
|
James Sisson
|
George Wing Sisson Sr.
|
George Wing Sisson Jr.
|
Stanley Sisson
|
David Sisson
|
Capt. Matthew Sisson

107

ADDENDUM #2: I'LL BE HOME FOR CHRISTMAS

I update my blog every year with this message:

My daughter Elizabeth would have turned 23 today, December 18, 2012. Expecting Elizabeth, due to be born on Christmas Eve of 1989, had been an exciting experience. But the moment she arrived on the 18th, I felt a stab of fear. My immediate thought was, "Her head looks so small—so deformed."

The neonatologist said, "Your daughter's brain is very small with calcium deposits throughout. If she lives, she will never roll over, sit up, or feed herself." He concluded that Elizabeth's birth defects were caused by congenital cytomegalovirus (CMV). Women who care for young children are at a higher risk for catching it because preschoolers are the majority of carriers. Pregnant women need to be careful not to kiss young children on or around the mouth or share food or towels with them.

Why hadn't my OB/GYN warned me about this?

While I was pregnant with Elizabeth, I not only had a toddler of my own, but I also ran a licensed daycare center in my home. I felt sick at what my lack of knowledge had done to my little girl. In milder cases, children with congenital CMV may lose hearing or struggle with learning disabilities later in life. But Elizabeth's case was not a mild one.

When my husband Jim heard Elizabeth's grim prognosis, he stared at her and said, "She needs me"—just like Charlie Brown with that pathetic Christmas tree.

It took me about a year, but I eventually stopped praying that a nuclear bomb would drop on my house so I could escape my overwhelming anguish over Elizabeth's condition. Life did become good again—but it took a lot of help from family, friends, and the Book of Psalms. We were eventually able to move forward as a happy, "normal" family.

Sixteen years later, I awoke feeling so proud of Elizabeth. It was her 16th birthday and just one week before her 17th Christmas. When the song "I'll be home for Christmas" played on the radio, I cried thinking how hard Elizabeth fought to be home with us, overcoming several battles with pneumonia, major surgeries, and most recently, seizures. Weighing only 50 pounds, she looked funny to strangers as a result of her small head and adult teeth, but she was lovely to us with her long, brown hair, large blue eyes and soul-capturing smile. Although still in diapers and unable to speak or hold up her head, Elizabeth was very happy and loved going for long car rides. She especially enjoyed going to school and being surrounded by people, paying no mind to the stares of "normal" children who thought she belonged on the "Island of Misfit Toys."

Less than two months after she turned 16, I dropped Elizabeth off at school. Strapping her into her wheelchair, I held her face in my hands, kissed her cheek, and said, "Now be a good girl today." She smiled as she heard her teacher say what she said every time, "Elizabeth is always a good girl!" With that, I left.

At the end of the day, I got the call I had always feared. "Mrs. Saunders, Elizabeth had a seizure and she's not breathing." The medical team did all they could, but she was gone.

While holding Elizabeth's body on his lap, my husband looked down into her partially open, lifeless eyes and cried, "No one is ever going to look at me again the way she did."

Now, as I prepare to celebrate my seventh Christmas without her, it is with some heartache that I bring down the holiday decorations from the attic. Elizabeth used to love to sit on the couch with her big, formerly homeless old dog Riley, and watch us decorate.

Now, I perform a new Christmas tradition. I carefully unfold the black and red checked shirt Elizabeth wore on her last day and hang it over an empty chair beside our fireplace. Although she can't be home for Christmas, I feel that she is my "Tiny Tim" who would say if she could, "God bless us, everyone!"

Although I miss Elizabeth, I'm glad she is free from suffering, glad she is safe in her new, Heavenly home. When my time comes, I will see her again.

The Only Thing I Can Do for Elizabeth Now

Since Elizabeth no longer needs my care, the only thing I can do for her now is to care for those not yet born—to prevent them from suffering as Elizabeth did. I do that by speaking and writing about congenital CMV prevention.

After presenting her life at the international Congenital CMV conference held at the Centers for Disease Control (CDC) in Atlanta, GA, in 2008, scientists from all over the world approached to thank me for inspiring them to continue their work.

Mothers, on the other hand, pushed their children towards me in wheelchairs and asked, "Why didn't my OB/GYN tell me how to prevent this?" One mother even asked, "Learning what you did, why didn't you do all you could to shout it from the rooftops?"

Until OB/GYNs make CMV prevention a standard practice of care, I'm trying to "shout it from the rooftops" through my memoir, *Anything But a Dog! The perfect pet for a girl with congenital CMV*. I hope to reach a general audience by sharing the unusual account of how a big, old homeless dog found his way to Elizabeth's couch. In the back of the book, I include CMV prevention and treatment tips from the country's leading CMV experts. It's available as an e-book or softcover and the first few chapters can be viewed for free online.

If a person would like a portion of the proceeds to be donated to CMV research and parent support, the soft cover version can be purchased through the National CMV Disease Registry at:

www.unlimitedpublishing.com/cmv

Please help prevent disease related birth defects by reviewing the CDC's fact sheet on preventing infections during pregnancy available at: http://www.cdc.gov/ncbddd/pregnancy_gateway/infections.html

ADDENDUM #3: WHAT SHOULD BE FAMOUS— AND ISN'T

"What you don't know can hurt your unborn baby"

Few women have heard of congenital CMV (cytomegalovirus) and more than half of OB/GYNs surveyed admitted they don't warn their patients about it.

According to the CDC:
- Every hour, congenital CMV causes one child to become disabled
- Each year, about 30,000 children are born with congenital CMV infection
- About 1 in 750 children is born with or develops permanent disabilities due to CMV
- About 8,000 children each year suffer permanent disabilities caused by CMV

The CDC makes the following recommendations on simple steps you can take to avoid exposure to saliva and urine that might contain CMV:

Wash your hands often with soap and water for 15-20 seconds, especially after
- changing diapers
- feeding a young child
- wiping a young child's nose or drool
- handling children's toys

In Addition:
- Do not share food, drinks, or eating utensils used by young children
- Do not put a child's pacifier in your mouth
- Do not share a toothbrush with a young child
- Avoid contact with saliva when kissing a child
- Clean toys, countertops, and other surfaces that come into contact with children's urine or saliva

To learn more about congenital CMV from the CDC, visit: cdc.gov/ncbddd/pregnancy_gateway/cmv/index.html

Congenital CMV Resources:

Congenital Cytomegalovirus Foundation—The mission of the Congenital CMV Foundation is to prevent birth defects resulting from congenital CMV infection. To contact leading congenital CMV experts, visit: http://www.congenitalcmv.org/foundation.htm

The National Congenital CMV Registry: The National Congenital CMV Disease Registry and Research Program in Houston, Texas, includes members from many disciplines and specialties who conduct clinical and laboratory research studies on congenital CMV disease, including ways to better define and promote awareness of the public health problem, the long term effects, and the treatment and prevention of congenital CMV disease. Visit them at: www.bcm.edu/pedi/infect/cmv

Stop CMV - The CMV Action Network:
The mission of Stop CMV - The CMV Action Network is to prevent and eliminate congenital CMV and to improve the lives of all people affected by congenital CMV. Since 2003, Stop CMV has been fostering congenital CMV awareness via internet and public awareness campaigns. The CMV Action Network is comprised of families, friends and medical professionals personally affected by CMV and committed to public education efforts to prevent future cases of the virus. Visit: StopCMV.org

Brendan B. McGinnis Congenital CMV Foundation—The non-profit organization is dedicated to raising awareness of CMV, to supporting CMV vaccine research, and to supporting families affected by CMV around the world. Visit: cmvfoundation.org

Congenital CMV Blog: http://congenitalcmv.blogspot.com
The author of this book, Lisa Saunders, maintains a congenital CMV blog and links to parent and media resources. Lisa's daughter Elizabeth was born severely affected by congenital CMV and died at the age of 16. Lisa is the author of the memoir, *Anything But a Dog! The perfect pet for a girl with congenital CMV,* and is available for speaking engagements. Contact her for her availability at saundersbooks@aol.com

Pirate sketch by Suzanne Doukas Niermeyer

MYSTIC SEAFARER'S TRAIL MAP

The Mystic Seafarer's Trail Map, which you see in the beginning of the book, was adapted from a map done by Constant Waterman, author of *Landmarks You Must Visit in Southeast Connecticut* (I highly recommend this book for those looking for information and exquisite pen and ink drawings on intriguing sites in the region). The Mystic Seafarer's Trail map is available for free printing at: mysticseafarerstrail.com

For those who love history or kayaking, visit the Mystic River Historical Society for their free walking and kayaking self-guided tours at: mystichistory.org/walking_tours.htm

Free tourist map available at: lighthousemaps.com/MysticIndex.html

Welcome Centers

Welcome Center at Mystic Depot
Greater Mystic Chamber of Commerce
2 Roosevelt Avenue (Route One), Mystic, CT 06355
860-572-9578, mysticchamber.org

Mystic & Shoreline Visitor Information Center
Olde Mistick Village, Mystic, CT 06355
860-536-1641, mysticinfocenter@yahoo.com
mysticinfo.com

Other good information available for tourists and locals:
- Mystic, Connecticut, mysticct.net
- Mystic Country Connecticut, mystic.org

Want to see Mystic before you get here?
You can hear and see local chefs, shop keepers and area merchants at: mysticshops.tv (where you can see Bailey in a dog walking commercial—he's the hound on your left), and at: mystv.com (where you can see my skirt in the casino commercial).

BIBLIOGRAPHY

"CAPTAIN NAT". (n.d.). Retrieved September 16, 2012, from Stonington Historical Society Nathaniel B. Palmer House : http://www.stoningtonhistory.org/palmer2.htm

THE BURNED STEAMER: MORE ACCOUNTS OF THE DISASTER. THE DESTRUCTION OF THE CITY OF WACO AT GALVESTON HOPELESS SEARCH FOR THE PASSENGERS AND CREW. CRUISE OF THE BUCKTHORN. FACTS AND CONCLUSIONS. LOCAL COMPANIES. CAPT. THOMAS WOLFE'S BODY TO BE SENT TO CONN. (1875, November 15). *The New York Times.*

THE CITY O THE CITY OF WACO.; THE BODY OF CAPT. WOLFE, THE GALVESTON PILOT, RECOVERED NO HOPE THAT ANY OF THOSE ON BOARD ESCAPED. (1875, November 14). *The New York Times.*

Lucien P. Smith's December Baby. (1912, December 28). *Sphere.* Retrieved September 16, 2012, from http://www.encyclopedia-titanica.org/lucien-p-smiths-december-baby.html

Rescue Ship Arrives--Thousands Gather At the Pier. (1912). *The New York Times.*

"BYRD PLIGHT IS REGARDED AS PERILOUS—Lives May Be Lost if Help Fails To Reach Them—HASTE IS IMPERATIVE—Ice Packs Threaten to Isolate Explorers With Food Supplies Running Low." . (1930, January 24). *Democrat and Chronicle*, pp. 1,20.

AMELIA EARHART WEDS G.P. PUTNAM. (1931, February 8). *The New York Times.*

Certificate of Marriage. (1931, February 7). Retrieved from Pres. Edward Elliot's Residence 1930-1940: http://earchives.lib.purdue.edu/cdm4/document.php?CISOROOT=/earhart&CISOPTR=3003&REC=1

US Army Survival Manual . (1991). New York: Dorset Press .

"The Leaving of Liverpool" Gaelic Mist . (2007, October 15). Retrieved September 16, 2012, from YouTube: http://www.youtube.com/watch?v=bdiLcJ14Mkc

Model 10 Electra. (2012, September 16). Retrieved from Lockheed Martin: http://www.lockheedmartin.com/us/100years/programs/model-10-electra.html

About Us: St. Edmund's Enders Island. (n.d.). Retrieved September 16, 2012, from St. Edmund's Enders Island at Mystic: https://www.endersisland.com/about-us

Acas, E. (2010, Fall). Marketing Communications Coordinator; Pelli Clarke Pelli Architects. (L. Saunders, Interviewer)

Adventure Town: Mystic, Conneciticut. (n.d.). Retrieved September 16, 2012, from National Georgraphic: http://adventure.nationalgeographic.com/adventure/trips/adventure-towns/mystic-connecticut/

AMELIA EARHART BIOGRAPHICAL SKETCH. (n.d.). Retrieved 2012, from Purdue University George Palmer Collections of Amelia Earhart Papers : http://www.lib.purdue.edu/spcol/aearhart/biography.php

Amelia Earhart--An American Hero. (n.d.). Retrieved September 22, 2012, from TheAvWriter: http://youtu.be/Qgk_zvpiIRw

Anderson, J. J. (2010, October 27). Executive Director, St. Edmunds Retreat, Enders Island. (L. Saunders, Interviewer)

Anderson, M. (2012, August). Curator, Noank Historical Society. (L. Saunders, Interviewer) Noank, Connecticut.

Anderson_Jr., R. P. (2012, September 26). Lawyer. (L. Saunders, Interviewer)

Baker, M. B. (2012, August 29). Director, Stonington Historical Society. (L. Saunders, Interviewer)

BATTISTA, C. (1987, November 01). FOR 'MYSTIC PIZZA,' TOWNS AND RESIDENTS 'JUST ACT NATURAL'. *The New York Times.*

Biography of Amelia Earhart. (n.d.). Retrieved September 16, 2012, from Amelia Earhart Birthplace Museum: http://www.ameliaearhartmuseum.org/AmeliaEarhart/AEBiography.htm

Blanch, L. M. (2010, 2012). Navy Community Liaison. (L. Saunders, Interviewer)

Bonfiglio, A. (2008, October 23-29). Dogs Have Their Day in the Sun. *Rockland County Times.* New York. Retrieved from http://myweb.ecomplanet.com/SAUN6703//Anything%20But%20a%20Dog%21%20Rockland%20County%20Times.pdf

Buffum_Jr., C. C. (2012, September 7). Owner, Cottrell Brewing Company. (L. Saunders, Interviewer)

Butler, S. (1999). Amelia Earhart. In *BOOKNOTES: Life Stories, Brian Lamb* (p. 238). New York: Three Rivers Press, Crown Publishing Group, National Cable Satellite Corporation.

Carter, M. W. (1973). *Shipswrecks and Marine Disasters on the Shores of The Town of Westerly, Rhode*

Island and Adjacent Waters. Shelter Harbor, Westerly, R.I.: David G. Carter.

Charles C. Sisson Papers (Coll. 114, Volume 6). (n.d.). Retrieved September 16, 2012, from Mystic Seaport: Museum of America and the Sea, Manuscript Collection Registers: http://library.mysticseaport.org/manuscripts/coll/coll114.cfm#restrictlink

Chick, L. (1989, Sept/Oct). Amelia Earhart: The reluctant bride married quietly in Noank. *Tidings--Retrieved from Noank Historical Society, Inc., Research Files*, p. 38.

CLASSIC CUISINE, HISTORIC GOOD TIME . (n.d.). Retrieved September 18, 2012, from Captain Daniel Packer Inne Restaurant and Pub: http://danielpacker.com/history.html

Cloutier, D. (. (2010, November 9). (L. Saunders, Interviewer)

Coleman, R. (2010, October 27). Bridgetender, Mystic River Bascule Bridge. (L. Saunders, Interviewer)

Collette, M. (2010, June 3). Amelia Earhart's connection to Noank commemorated. *The Day- -Retrieved from Noank Historical Society, Inc., Research Files*.

Comrie, M. J. (1981, April 15). *Elm Grove Cemetary Association History*. Retrieved September 16, 2012, from Elm Grove Cemetary: http://elmgrovecemetery.org/history.pdf

Connecticut State Department of Health. (1930, November 8). Marriage License. Groton, Connecticut.

Crawford, T. (2012). Master of Otto the Dog. (L. Saunders, Interviewer)

Cunningham, T. (2012, September 10). President of the Greater Mystic Chamber of Commerce. (L. Saunders, Interviewer)

Cutler, C. C. (1930). *Greyhounds of the Sea: The Story of the American Clipper Ship*. G.P. Putnam's Sons.

Davis, J. (FAll 2010). Superintendent, Elm Grove Cemetary. (L. Saunders, Interviewer)

Denk, R. (1990). *The Complete Sailing Handbook*. London: Tiger Books International PLC.

Descendants of Richard (1608-1684) and Mary (d. 1692) SISSON of Rhode Island, Eight Generation. (n.d.). Retrieved September 19, 2012, from Rootsweb: http://homepages.rootsweb.ancestry.com/~dasisson/richard/aqwg114.htm#322 18

Descendants of Richard (1608-1684) and Mary (d. 1692) SISSON of Rhode Island, Ninth Generation. (n.d.). Retrieved September 19, 2012, from Rootsweb: http://homepages.rootsweb.ancestry.com/~dasisson/richard/aqwg172.htm#322 25

Dombrowski, S. (2010, November 12). Hilton. (L. Saunders, Interviewer)

Dorothy Putnam. (n.d.). Retrieved from St. Lucie Historical Society, Inc.:
http://martincountydemocr.easycgi.com/stlucie/dorothyputnam.htm

Earhart, A. (1931, February 7). *Letter, 1931 Feb. 7, Noank, Conn., to GPP (draft).* Retrieved
from Pres. Edward Elliot's Residence 1930-1940:
http://earchives.lib.purdue.edu/cdm4/document.php?CISOROOT=/earhart&CI
SOPTR=2999&REC=16

Earhart, A. (n.d.). *Letter_2901 Caption: Letter from Amelia Earhart to Byrd, July 30, 1928, Richard
E. Byrd Papers, #2901. Amelia Earhart pledged not only her good wishes, but also money she
earned from a cigarette ad, to Byrd's Antarctic Expedition.* Retrieved September 18, 2012,
from Ohio State University Libraries, Conquering the Ice: Byrd's Flight to the
South Pole: http://library.osu.edu/projects/conquering-the-
ice/LETTER_2901.jpg

(n.d.). Ecclesiastes 1:6. In *Bible.*

Elgen M. Long and Marie K. Long. (1999). *Amelia Earhart: The Mystery Solved.* New York:
Simon & Schuster.

Employee, F. (2010). Behind front desk, Whaler's Inn, Mystic, CT. (L. Saunders,
Interviewer)

Encyclopedia Titanic. (n.d.). Lucian Philip Smith. Retrieved from http://www.encyclopedia-
titanica.org/titanic-victim/lucian-philip-smith.html

Encyclopedia Titanica. (n.d.). Mary Eloise Smith. Retrieved September 16, 2012, from
http://www.encyclopedia-titanica.org/titanic-survivor/mary-eloise-smith.html

Estate of John E. McDonald, D. (1930, May 1). Administrator's Deed. Groton, Connecticut,
United States.

Fagin, S. (1979, February). Spirit of Amelia Earhart still flies high in Noank. *New London Day-
-Retrieved from Noank Historical Society, Inc., Research Files,* pp. 1,20.

Fought, L. (2007). *A History of Mystic Connecticut: From Pequot Village to Tourist Town.*
Charleston, SC: History Press.

From Our Special Reporters. (1876, July 5). *Norwich Courier.* Retrieved May 17, 2013, from
Geneologybank.com.

G., S. (2010, November 5). Waitress, Mystic Pizza. (L. Saunders, Interviewer)

German, A. W. (2005). *Mystic Seaport: A Visitor's Guide* . Mystic, CT: Mystic Seaport.

Gilmartin, G. (2010, November 9). Owner, Mystv Studios. (L. Saunders, Interviewer)

Ginger Rogers: The Official Site. (n.d.). Retrieved from
    http://www.gingerrogers.com/about/quotes.html

Goodman, M. V. (circa 1971). *Noank Notes.* Noank, Connecticut: Found in Noank Historical
    Society, Inc., Research Files.

Gordinier, G. S. (2012). *The Rockets' Red Glare: The War of 1812 and Connecticut.* New London,
    CT: New London Historical Society.

Grant, R. (2002). *Flight: 100 Years of Aviation.* New York: DK Publising, Inc.

Grimes, W. (2007, July 20). Beyond 'Moby-Dick': When America Went A-Fishing for the
    Whale. *The New York Times.*

Hall, N. (1995, March 26). Amelia Earhart grounded long enough to get married in Noank.
    Norwich Bulletin--Retrieved from Noank Historical Society, Inc., Research Files.

Hanna, D. (2012, September 14). Collections Manager, Mystic River Historical Society. (L.
    Saunders, Interviewer)

Historians Corner. (n.d.). *The Sisson Stones.* Mystic River Historical Society.

In Memoriam: Drowned off Galveston Bar...Steamer City of Waco...Capt. Thomas Eldredge
    Wolfe...Inquest. (n.d.). *Retrieved from Mystic River Historical Society.*

(n.d.). John 3:8. In *Bible.*

John Bishop Putnam. (n.d.). Retrieved from wikepedia:
    http://en.wikipedia.org/wiki/John_Bishop_Putnam

Johnson, J. (2011). Director, Marketing and Communications, Denison Pequotsepos Nature
    Center. (L. Saunders, Interviewer)

Joshua Piven and David Borgenicht. (1999). *The Worst-Case Scenerio Survival Handbook.* Quirk
    Productions.

Katie Bradford, M. (2012, September). Owner, Custom Marine Canvas. (L. Saunders,
    Interviewer)

Kimball, C. W. (2002, January 17). Capt. Thomas E. Wolfe of Mystic lived life to the hilt. *The
    Day*, p. Retrieved from Mystic River Historical Socieity.

Kimball, C. W. (2005). *Historic Glimpses: recollections of days past in the Mystic River Valley.* Mystic,
    Connecticut: Flat Hammock Press.

King, J. (2011, August 31). *Groton Respite Center Wants Town, Region To Take Showers .* Retrieved
    from Groton Patch: http://groton.patch.com/articles/groton-respite-center-
    wants-town-region-to-take-showers

King, J. (2011, March 6). *Project Oceanology Seal Cruise (with Video)*. Retrieved September 16, 2011, from New London Patch: http://montville-ct.patch.com/articles/project-oceanology-seal-cruise-with-video-3#video-5155164

Leavitt, J. F. (1973). *The Charles W. Morgan.* Mystic, Connecticut: Mystic Seaport, The Marine Historical Association, Incorporated.

Leslie, E. E. (1988). *Desperate Journeys, Abandoned Souls: True stories of casaways and other survivors.* Boston: Houghton Mifflin Company.

Life Book's. (2000). The Greatest Adventures of All Time. Time Inc. Home Entertainment.

Lockett, B. J. (2009). *Mystic Connecticut: A Woman's Hundred Year Journy to Heaven.* Mystic: Life's Journey Publishing Co. .

Long, E. M. (1999). *Amelia Earhart: The Mystery Solved.* New York: Touchstone.

Marshall, B. T. (1922). *A modern history of New London County, Connecticut.* Lewis Historical Publishing Company.

McDowell, L. R. (2013). *Vitamin History, the early years.* E-book (in press).

McFadden, D. (2012, August 9). Director of Communications, Mystic Seaport: The Museum of American and the Sea. (L. Saunders, Interviewer)

McManus, M. M. (2012, July). *Researchers Searching For Amelia Earhart's Plane Wreckage Sail From Hawaii To Nikumaroro.* Retrieved August 2012, from Huffington Post: http://www.huffingtonpost.com/2012/07/03/amelia-earhart-search-hawaii-nikumaroro_n_1648117.html

Melville, H. (1851). *Moby Dick, or, the whale.*

Mercer, K. (2011). *Shari's Pet Sitting Service.* Retrieved September 16, 2012, from MysticShops.TV: http://mysticshops.tv/shari-pet-sitting

Merz, E. (2012, September 5). Communications, Mystic Aquarium. (L. Saunders, Interviewer)

Mill, J. (1976, November 12). Residents recall Earhart Wedding. *THE NEWS--Retrieved from Noank Historical Society, Inc., Research Files.*

Mystic Pizza: 20th Anniversary Movie Trail. (n.d.). Retrieved September 16, 2012, from http://www.mysticchamber.org/doc/1/Mystic%20Pizza%20Movie%20Trail%20-%20Web.pdf

Mystic River Historical Society. (n.d.). *A Kayakers' Guide to the Mystic River & Its History.* Mystic, Connecticut: Louis Allyn.

Mystic River Historical Society. (1995). *Curbstones, Clapboards and Cupolas.* Mystic Rivers Historical Society.

Mystic River Historical Society. (2004). *Images of America Mystic* . Arcadia Publishing.

Mystic River Historical Society. (2010). *Colors of Mystic.* Mystic: Mystic River Historical Society.

Mystic River Historical Society. (n.d.). *About Us.* Retrieved September 25, 2012, from Mystic River Historical Society: http://www.mystichistory.org/about_mrhs.htm

Mystic River Historical Society. (n.d.). Mystic River Walking Adventure. Retrieved from www.mystichistory.org/MRHSTourGravelnobg_72dpi.pdf

Nair, M. (Director). (2009). *Amelia* [Motion Picture].

Peterson, B. (2010, November 17). Mystic Historian. (L. Saunders, Interviewer)

Peterson, W. N. (1989). *"Mystic Built": Ships and Shipyards of the Mystic River, 1784-1919.* . Mystic : Mystic Seaport Museum.

Peterson, W. N. (1998). The Wartime Shipbuilding Boom at Mystic, Connecticut. In W. M. Benjamin W. Labaree, *American and the Sea: A Maritime History* (pp. 358-359). Mystic, CT: Mystic Seaport.

Reardon, N. (2010, November 18). Landscape Unlimited, Stonington, CT (client: Elm Grove Cemetary). (L. Saunders, Interviewer)

Records of the bark Marques (Coll. 244). (n.d.). Retrieved September 16, 2012, from Mystic Seaport: The Museum of American and the Sea, Manuscript Collection Registers: http://library.mysticseaport.org/manuscripts/coll/coll244.cfm

Reed, F. (2012, August 27). Manager of NavList . (L. Saunders, Interviewer)

Richard, E. (2010, October 21). Communications. (L. Saunders, Interviewer)

Robert P. Anderson, Jr. (November 17, 2010). *Amelia Earhart in Noank.* Retrieved from Noank Historical Society, Inc., Research Files: Paper given to Ariston Club, New London, and Noank Historical Society.

Robertson, C. H. (2012, September 4). Olde Mistick Village. (L. Saunders, Interviewer)

Santos, T. (2009). *Mystic in the 1950s: Growing Up in a Small Village.*

Saunders, L. (1995). *Ride a Horse Not an Elevator.* Lisa Saunders.

Saunders, L. (2004). *Ever True: A Union Private and His Wife.* Maryland: Heritage Books.

Saunders, L. (2009). *Anything But a Dog! The perfect pet for a girl with congenital CMV (cytomegalovirus)*. Unlimited Publishing LLC.

Saunders, L. (2010, December 16). Gloria the goose survives to see another Christmas. *Mystic River Press.*

Saunders, L. (2011, January 4). *Cast Your Vote For The Eighth Wonder Of Mystic.* Retrieved from Stonington-Mystic Patch: http://stonington.patch.com/articles/cast-your-vote-for-the-eighth-wonder-of-mystic

Saunders, L. (2011). *Cindy Modzelewski gives a kayak launching lesson .* Retrieved from YouTube--LisaSaundersCom: http://www.youtube.com/user/LisaSaundersCom?feature=mhee#p/u/5/oQDO q9eiLsw

Saunders, L. (2011, March-April). Hey, Harbor Seals--Move Over! *the Resident.*

Saunders, L. (2011, August 5). *Kate and Bailey at Ford's Lobster.* Retrieved October 1, 2012, from YouTube--LisaSaundersCom: http://www.youtube.com/watch?v=r6XAMY65Mi0&list=UUy2jnwG7JbVjzT3p pPEjqHw&index=4&feature=plcp

Saunders, L. (2011). *Shays' Rebellion: The Hanging of Co-Leader, Captain Henry Gale.* Connecticut: Lisa Saunders.

Saunders, L. (2011). *The 7 Wonders of Mystic--Mystic Pizza and Beyond!* Lisa Saunders.

Scotti, R. (2003). *Sudden Sea: The Great Hurricane of 1938.* Boston, New York, London: Little, Brown and Company.

Servidio, B. (2012, August 26). Confirmed Facts. (L. Saunders, Interviewer)

Shanghai--Definition of. (n.d.). Retrieved October 2, 2012, from oxforddictionaries.com: http://oxforddictionaries.com/definition/american_english/shanghai?region=us &q=shanghaiing

Stackpole, M. (2011, November 5). Ship's Historian. (L. Saunders, Interviewer)

Sullivan, B. (. (2010, October 2010). Bridgetender, Mystic River Bascule Bridge. (L. Saunders, Interviewer)

The Earhart Project. (n.d.). Retrieved September 16, 2012, from The International Group for Historic Aircraft Recovery (TIGHAR): http://tighar.org/Projects/Earhart/Archives/Research/Bulletins/63_DebrisField /63_DebrisField.htm

The International Group for Historical Aircraft Recovery. (n.d.). Retrieved August 2012, from TIGHAR: http://tighar.org/

The Morgan in the Movies. (n.d.). Retrieved September 16, 2012, from Mystic Seaport: Museum
    of America and the Sea:
    http://www.mysticseaport.org/index.cfm?fuseaction=home.viewPage&page_id=
    B61320D3-65B8-D398-7A1BB0E4609C4E5C

Washington Potatoes Are Nutritious. (n.d.). Retrieved September 17, 2012, from Washington
    State Potatoe Commission: http://potatoes.com/Nutrition.cfm

Waterman, C. (2010). *Landmarks You Must Visit In Southeast Connecticut.* Mystic, Connecticut:
    Matthew Goldman aka Constant Waterman.

Willaim P. Muttart, Linda R. Ashley. (2006). *One Hundred & Eleven Questions & Answers
    Concerning the Pilgrims: Passengers on the Mayflower, 1620.* Montville, CT: Mayflower
    Books.

Wilson, J. &. (1982, October-November). Amelia's Last Flight. *Modern Maturity--Retrieved from
    Noank Historical Society, Inc., Research Files.*

Young, S. (1970, November 11). Amelia Earhart Made News in Noank. *The Day--Retrieved
    from Noank Historical Society, Inc., Research Files,* p. 40.

Zelepos, J. (2010, November 9). Owner, Mystic Pizza. (L. Saunders, Interviewer)

INDEX

ENDNOTES

[i] Lou Allyn was raised in Mystic and attended schools on both sides of the river and retired "back home" to Masons Island in 1998. Mystic and its history has always been a love of his, along with the Great Hurricane of 1938. His family tree includes great grandfather Louis Allyn who built the house on the northeast corner of Allyn Street and New London Road and grandmother Laura Greenman. (He remembers visiting the aunts and uncles at the George Greenman house and marveled that they had a real whaling ship at the end of their vegetable garden.) Lou Allyn is active in the Mystic River Historical Society and several other community organizations in Mystic..

[ii] (McDowell, 2013)

[iii] (Young, 1970)

[iv] Self-guided walking tour available free at:
http://www.mystichistory.org/MRHSWalkTourJan11a.pdf

[v] For more locations of the Mystic Community Bikes, visit: mysticcommunitybikes.org. The mission of the Mystic Community Bikes is to facilitate bicycling in the Mystic community by providing and maintaining bicycles for public use.

[vi] (King, Project Oceanology Seal Cruise (with Video), 2011)

[vii] (CLASSIC CUISINE, HISTORIC GOOD TIME)

[viii] (Discovering Titanic)

[ix] (Buffum Jr., 2012)

[x] (Long & Long, 1999, p. 42)

[xi] (Encyclopedia Titanic)
(Lucien P. Smith's December Baby, 1912)

[xii] My friend Pam came up with that term, "Hallmark Move," for life in Mystic, but I like to pretend I did.

[xiii] (Saunders, Cindy Modzelewski gives a kayak launching lesson , 2011)

[xiv] A Kayakers' Guide to the Mystic River & Its History is available at Bank Square Books and Mystic River Historical Society's Downes Building in heavy, waterproof coated paper.

Also available as a free pdf at: http://www.mystichistory.org/tours/kayakers_guide.pdf

^{xv} That misadventure is told in my memoir, *Anything But a Dog!*

^{xvi} To learn more about Elizabeth's life and how to prevent congenital cytomegalovirus (CMV) from happening to other children, see Addendum #2 and #3.

^{xvii} Available free at: http://www.mystichistory.org/tours/curbstones_booklet.pdf

^{xviii} See Addendum I

^{xix} As boys, they most likely attended Portersville Academy. Built in 1839, Portersville Academy was purchased by the Mystic River Historical Society from the Town of Groton, restored, and is used an outreach and educational space. It is located on High Street in Mystic, south of West Main Street. Adjacent to it is the William A. Downes Building, which houses the Mystic River Historical Society's Archives and Offices. Self-guided walking and kayaking tours are available for free at: http://www.mystichistory.org/walking_tours.htm

^{xx} Lat. 12 degrees 00' North, Long. 39 degrees 30' West

^{xxi} (Charles C. Sisson Papers (Coll. 114, Volume 6, pg 293)

^{xxii} (Charles C. Sisson Papers (Coll. 114, Volume 6, pg 294)

^{xxiii} (Charles C. Sisson Papers (Coll. 114, Volume 6, pg 303)

^{xxiv} (Charles C. Sisson Papers (Coll. 114, Volume 6, pg 309)

^{xxv} (Cutler, 1930, pg 313)

^{xxvi} (Gordinier, 2012)

^{xxvii} ("CAPTAIN NAT")

^{xxviii} ("The Leaving of Liverpool" Gaelic Mist , 2007)

^{xxix} See Addendum #3 : What Should be Famous—but isn't

^{xxx} Though not an overly dramatic hurricane, Hurricane Floyd was a terror for me because I was trapped on a train in New Jersey with our disabled daughter, Elizabeth. Although there were there were fun moments like the woman screaming hysterically in the snack bar because the waiter had run out of biscottis, the rest of the trip was tense as I replayed in my mind how best to keep Elizabeth from drowning if we had to swim for it through the ever-rising water around us. Although Elizabeth was nine at the time, she was unable to walk, sit up, or eat anything but pureed food. I also had to figure out how to get her some food. I hadn't packed much in my bag since it was only intended to be a three-hour train trip. Now it was nearing 10 hours. Two passengers babysat Elizabeth so I could walk up and down the aisles begging people for their containers of yogurt because she needed something smooth to eat. I offered my cookies in trade for the yogurt—and it worked. Amazed by my armful of yogurts, an old man snapped my photo. (Note to self: always keep cookies on hand—you never know when you need to eat or trade them.) Passenger civility toward one another, however, dissolved when the train was finally able to move forward to a location where buses were sent to help us complete our trip. Now, it was everyman for himself. Passengers pushed ahead of us in order to escape the misery as each bus arrived. We missed bus after bus, which meant Elizabeth had to sit in the pouring rain in her wheelchair for a very long time. Several buses later, a bus driver saw what was going on. He got out of his seat and pushed his way towards us through the angry crowd. Without saying a word to me, he lifted Elizabeth out of her wheelchair and carried her onboard. I yelled after him, "Please be careful, she can't sit up by herself." When I finally made it through the crowd with her wheelchair and my luggage, I saw that the bus driver had enlisted the help of passengers to hold her up in a seat. The bus driver diverted from his scheduled route to take us exactly where we needed to go. Now, more than a decade later, I still feel thankful for that bus driver, whose name I wish I knew.

^{xxxi} (Ginger Rogers: The Official Site)

^{xxxii} When Jackie came home from college to meet Bailey for the first time, she took him to Harriman State Park. Later, I got a call. "Mom," she said, "There was a man standing among the trees who kept staring at Bailey. He didn't move a muscle the entire 10 minutes I was

there--it was really creepy." I replied, "He was probably deciding how much of a threat Bailey would be if he attacked you. You better call the police since he gave you such a weird feeling." The day after she reported him, a policeman called her back and told her to come into the Bear Mountain police station, which was 45 minutes away, to make a formal statement. The next day, Jackie went to the police station. The officer asked her questions and typed her responses into his computer. Finishing up his questioning, he asked, "Why did you call the police to report this man staring at your dog." My 20-year-old replied, "Because my mother made me." The officer typed that too. Then, he finally told Jackie why she had been called in. Jackie called me at work. "Mom, that man was dead when the police got there. When they found him, he was hanging in the trees from a noose around his neck. I just couldn't tell because there was a rise of earth in front of his feet. He had his wallet on him so they were able to identify him. They told me I was lucky I hadn't approached him, because then my footprints would have launched a murder investigation."

[xxxiii] (Saunders, Shays' Rebellion: The Hanging of Co-Leader, Captain Henry Gale, 2011)
[xxxiv] (Saunders, Gloria the goose survives to see another Christmas, 2010)
[xxxv] http://polldaddy.com/poll/4338240/
[xxxvi] http://stonington.patch.com/articles/cast-your-vote-for-the-eighth-wonder-of-mystic
[xxxvii] First chapter of *Anything But a Dog!* is available for free viewing at: www.authorlisasaunders.com
[xxxviii] (Mercer, 2011)
[xxxix]

http://www.youtube.com/watch?v=r6XAMY65Mi0&list=UUy2jnwG7JbVjzT3ppPEjqHw&index=4&feature=plcp
[xl] (Robert P. Anderson, Jr., November 17, 2010)
[xli] (Dorothy Putnam)
[xlii] (AMELIA EARHART BIOGRAPHICAL SKETCH)
[xliii] (Butler, 1999, p. 238)
[xliv] (Long & Long, 1999, p. 37)
[xlv] (Chick, 1989, p. 40)
[xlvi] http://memory.loc.gov/service/mss/eadxmlmss/eadpdfmss/2003/ms003068.pdf Library of Congress: The papers of Nathaniel Brown Palmer and other family members were deposited in the Library of Congress in several installments between 1927 and 1937 by Elizabeth Dixon (Mrs. Richard Fanning) Loper, Alexander Palmer Loper, and other members of the Loper family. These deposits were later converted to gifts and purchases. Additional papers were Palmer-Loper Family Papers given to the Library by Alexander P. Loper in 1938-1939, and by Harriet B. Brown, Malcolm F. Brown, and Mark Palmer between 1992 and 2000.
[xlvii] (Long & Long, 1999, p. 40)
[xlviii] (Amelia Earhart--An American Hero)
[xlix] (Earhart, Letter_2901 Caption: Letter from Amelia Earhart to Byrd, July 30, 1928, Richard E. Byrd Papers, #2901.)
[l] (Mill, 1976)
[li] (Mill, 1976)
[lii] (Chick, 1989)
[liii] (Earhart, Letter, 1931 Feb. 7, Noank, Conn., to GPP (draft), 1931)
[liv] (Mill, 1976)
[lv] (Robert P. Anderson, Jr., November 17, 2010)
[lvi] (Mill, 1976)
[lvii] (Mill, 1976)
[lviii] (AMELIA EARHART WEDS G.P. PUTNAM, 1931)
[lix] (Mill, 1976)

[lx] (Chick, 1989)

[lxi] (Mill, 1976)

[lxii] (Mill, 1976)

[lxiii] (Mill, 1976)

[lxiv] (Mary Virginia Goodman, circa 1971)

[lxv] (AMELIA EARHART WEDS G.P. PUTNAM, 1931)

[lxvi] (Robert P. Anderson, Jr., November 17, 2010)

[lxvii] (AMELIA EARHART BIOGRAPHICAL SKETCH)

[lxviii] (Life Book's, 2000)

[lxix] (AMELIA EARHART BIOGRAPHICAL SKETCH)

[lxx] (Wilson, 1982)

[lxxi] (Fagin, 1979)

[lxxii] (Collette, 2010)

[lxxiii] (The International Group for Historical Aircraft Recovery)

[lxxiv] (McManus, 2012)

[lxxv] http://www.youtube.com/watch?v=rGX8jPMRp5M

[lxxvi] http://www.mysticshops.tv/shari-pet-sitting/

[lxxvii] See Addendum #2: "I'll Be Home For Christmas"

[lxxviii] Ever True: A Civil War Love Story, Valentine's Day (Feb 14, 2012):The love letters of a private and his 17-year-old wife reveal dreams, desertions, disease, hangings, and the court marshaling of a cow. Presented by the Emerson Theater Collaborative with real actors (instead of me, at 50, playing the part of the 17-year-old), I was thrilled at how the audience of military families experienced it. One woman wrote to me, *"Ever True held a particular sensibility for us because, as we listened to the young actors reading the letters of Mr. and Mrs. McDowell, we were reminded of the letters we sent to one another during 1970. When you're in love and separated at the beginning of your marriage and are as insecure as we were about whether our love would sustain us through these 13 months, there is vulnerability for both the man and woman. The actors captured that vulnerability as well as the sadness, bitterness, and anger that we also felt going through that time. Greg turned to me when the play was finished and we held each other's hand. No words needed to be spoken in that moment because we each understood that Ever True captured our experience and the love we had back then, which is only stronger today."*—Peggy Jordan

[lxxix] From a headstone at Wichtman burying ground in Old Mystic, Connecticut, in memory of Captain Elijah B. Morgan of the ship *Contest*. He died at sea off the coast of Brazil in 1861.